MW00929273

Behind Shooters Bar

by

Kay Derr

DISCLAIMER

I have tried to recreate events, locales, and conversations from my memories of them. In order to maintain their anonymity in some instances, I have changed the names of individuals and places. I may have changed some identifying characteristics and details such as physical properties, occupation, and places of residences.

DEDICATION

This book is dedicated, posthumously, to my natural father and mother whom I never had the privilege of knowing.

MY LEGACY

May my story be a legacy for my grandchildren: Gary, Charissa, John, Matthew, and Madelyn. And, for my great-grandchildren: Dominik, Troy, Delavan, Ryleigh, Briar and those yet future.

Copyright Kay Derr 2018

Published in the United States of America

First Edition: 2018

All rights reserved. No portion of this book may be reproduced or transmitted in any form or by any electronic or mechanical means, including photocopying, recording or by an information retrieval and storage system without the permission of the publisher.

E books are not transferable, either in whole or part. As the purchaser or otherwise lawful recipient of this book, you have the right to enjoy the book on your computer or other devices. Further distribution, copying, sharing, gifting or uploading is illegal and violates the United States Copyright Laws.

Printing of e books is illegal. Criminal Copyright Infringement, including infringement without monetary gain, may be investigated by the Federal Bureau of investigation and is punishable by, up to five years in federal prison and a fine of up to $250,000.

INTRODUCTION

Years ago I was speaking at a restaurant near Albany, New York. I had noticed the young waiter had been listening. Later he asked, "How is it you can stand here and tell your story?" He was gracious and genuinely sincere.

How could I tell my story? Never would I have wanted to unlock the pain of my past. Yet I neither wanted to waste it nor did I want to die with the music still inside. The music is my song of victory. I have overcome and I owe it all to the Master Healer, my Savior, Jesus Christ.

I tell my story because I believe there are thousands, even millions, who are struggling to find a way out of their own darkness. If you are going through troublesome times, tragedies, or trials, there is hope. Jesus has promised, "For I know the plans I have for you…plans to prosper you and not to harm you, plans to give you hope and a future." Jeremiah 29:11

ACKNOWLEDGEMENTS

Endless thanks to my heavenly Father who knew me from the beginning and orchestrated my life. Despite years of procrastination in writing this book God reminded me daily how to share His love, forgiveness, protection, and salvation story. I'm extremely grateful that He came by my side and buoyed me on when the tears flowed.

I would like to thank my adoptive parents, posthumously, for loving my sister and me unconditionally.

A special thanks to Muriel Shaffer who was instrumental in helping to edit my book. Coincidently, Muriel once lived on the second floor of Shooters Bar.

I am humbled and grateful for June Bryan Belfie my hometown mentor and encourager. June's adventurous spirit shines brightly through every page of her Amish novels.

Millions of thanks to Florence Littauer whom without her Christian Leaders Authors and Speakers Seminars I would not have learned the value of sharing my story.

A bouquet of roses to Marilyn Willett Heavilin who, along with her husband Glen, shared their experiences of grief and loss. She writes: "I first met Kay Derr at a Christian Booksellers Association conference over thirty years ago. Kay was a version of SAD. I tried to encourage her. I learned later that my book did what I couldn't do. My book, *Roses in December*, gave Kay hope and encouragement when she needed it!" Marilyn Heavilin

My heart still smiles when I think of my dear friend, now with the Lord, Nancy Dorner from Kalamazoo, Michigan. Nancy taught me valuable lessons in speaking to a crowd, how to write right, and above all else how to laugh.

Last, but not least, I would like to thank my sons, Greg and Gary. I am grateful, in the absence of their dad, that they love me enough to have wished to spare my reliving the past over the writing journey.

TABLE OF CONTENTS

Hobos, the Rag Man, and the Skunk Farm

Hidden in a dresser drawer of my childhood home was a family heirloom passed down through generations. Little had I known this rustic relic would forever change the direction of my life.

The home was my paternal grandparents' located in the second ward in small-town Danville, Pennsylvania. It was nestled on a triangular plot next to a stately red brick house. More like a shack than a house, the clapboards had never been painted resulting in a mishmash of varied shades of brown. It was, however, surrounded by a picket fence which enhanced its otherwise drab alley view. Hollyhocks in an array of pinks, whites, reds, and yellows danced along the fence. Fragrant blue sweet peas perfumed the air. Pink bleeding hearts and varicolored bearded iris brightened the landscape.

The tiny abode was dwarfed by a massive maple tree, providing an umbrella of shade over the house. A barn at the rear of the home had also never been painted. During the summertime, a small garden yielded sweet corn for the family

at a time when World War II was escalating. My parents
lived there with my paternal grandparents and Kenneth Lee, my
brother. It was 1943. Three years earlier my family buried our
older sister, Caroline Eugenia, who was born and died of
pneumonia that same year. I, Sylvia Kay, came along in
1941. Our sister, Linda Lee, was born in 1942.

At twenty-two months of age, I could not have known that one
day my sister and I would not live in that house and, in fact, no
longer be a member of our natural family. Neither would we
live in Danville but would grow up in a sister town—Riverside.

The two boroughs were separated by the Susquehanna River
that snaked through the valley and, ultimately, emptied into the
Chesapeake Bay. In its early history, Indians trailed the river
banks leaving behind relics which are a part of Montour
County's rich historical collection.

In 1845 skilled immigrants from Ireland, England, Germany,
and Wales populated our town and mined ore from the
surrounding hills. The ore was converted to iron in the Big Mill;
thus our village became known as an iron town. The first iron T-
rail was rolled in Danville, having set the pattern for America's
railroads.

By 1853, Danville had three rolling mills producing T-rails,
five blast furnaces, and four foundries. With the 1873
depression and the country's conversion from iron to steel,
however, the iron industry began to decline. In 1895, the early
ironworks were consolidated into two firms: The Reading
Iron Company, operating the Big Mill, and the Glendower
Iron Works. The mills continued to run through the turn of the
century, with the Big Mill ceasing operation at the end of the
Great Depression.

The Montour County Courthouse was erected in 1871 and the Geisinger Memorial Hospital in Danville in 1915 in honor of Abigail Geisinger's iron-magnate husband, George F. The hospital was founded on the principles of the Bible and with the mandate that the Geisinger name never be removed. Today the hospital is a sprawling medical complex and the largest employer in the Susquehanna Valley, including multiple hospitals and Geisinger office buildings throughout the northeast.

My paternal ancestry began with Johann Philip Beyer who was born March 23, 1701, in Flomersheim, Frankenthal, Rhineland-Palatinate, Germany and died in Amity, Berks County, Pennsylvania on May 7, 1753. While I have been able to trace the Beyer family roots to Valten Beyer, who was born in Germany in 1435 and died in 1520, Johann Philip was the first Beyer to have immigrated to America.

Johann came to America on the ship *Pennsylvania Merchant*, which landed at Philadelphia on September 11, 1731. With him came his wife and children. They settled first in Frederick Township, Montgomery County, Pennsylvania, but soon moved into Oley Township, and finally into Amity Township, Berks County. He was a member of the Falckner Swamp Lutheran Church where five of his children were confirmed the Sunday after Easter, 1746, by the Patriarch Henry M. Muhlenberg and became identified early with the Old Goshenhoppen Lutheran Church. He reportedly died in 1753 and was buried at the Swamp Lutheran Church cemetery. Reverend Henry Melchior Muhlenberg, for whom Muhlenberg College in Allentown, Pennsylvania was named, officiated his burial.

My adoptive parents moved with my sister and me from Danville to Avenue E in Riverside. We lived in a mirror image duplex on a corner lot. A short time later the Kolenda family moved to the other side of the house. Adding to the double anomaly of the home was the fact that both moms were named Grace. My dad's name was Joseph and, even though he was never overweight, was nicknamed Chub.

My sister and I now had playmates; two boys and a girl who came along later. From the street view, a mature maple tree could be seen on each side of the duplex. A gutter ran from "our" tree down to the cross-wise street. In the summertime, I loved floating my faded yellow and red wooden boats down the stream.

Dad had a black car with a crank starter. I'm not sure what year the car was and, in fact, I don't know the model. But if memory serves me correctly, it had one of those fold-up hoods. I remember sitting in the front seat of that old relic on a freezing cold day under the giant leafless maple tree. I can still see the black-knobbed gearshift sticking out of the floor next to me as I shivered waiting for Dad to get to the car. Finally, he grabbed the crank and began cranking at the front of the car. When the stubborn thing refused to start…well I won't tell you what he did with the crank, but it was accompanied by a string of strange words.

Directly in front of the matching porches of our house stood twin cedar trees. Our porch had a long wooden swing hung by chains. As kids, we rocked the swing from side to side. It was a real tummy thrill to sweep up over the banister. Surprisingly, no one ever got hurt.

The lazy days of summertime on Avenue E were marvelous. I was intrigued by the "iron man." Peddling a cart, the iron man was somewhat a collector of people's junk for which was the recycling of the day. He'd drive up the street at a snail's pace calling out "Rags…iron." Many folks who grew up in Riverside still have fond memories of the iron man.

Homeless vagrants also called tramps or hobos, shacked up in railroad boxcars. Whenever a train stopped on the tracks that stretched through Riverside, the unfortunate men roamed the streets looking for a handout. Our neighbor, Mrs. Johnson, kept a table on her back porch for those "bumming" for food. She'd serve them; then they returned to the rails. Though smelly, dirty, and ragged, we kids never feared the bums. We were intrigued by them! No doubt about it, when spotted, one of us alerted, "Here comes a bum!"

Along our side of the house was a row of red currant bushes. I could never resist sampling the luscious berries when they had ripened. In our backyard, a giant old apple tree grew producing sickly inedible fruit in the summertime. The tree must've been a hundred years old, but it was strong enough to hold a kid on a rope swing. As a pre-teen, I loved to stand on the swing with my younger cousin, Larry, perched on the seat. I recall crooning, "Irene, goodnight, Irene" as we lilted back and forth.

Not far from the apple tree stood our weathered two-seater outhouse. Piled next to the seats were all manner of newspaper pages and a Sears catalog. Toilet paper hadn't yet become a commodity in most homes back in the early 1940s. I remember stuffing the knot holes with paper so that a particular neighborhood boy wouldn't peek through while I was in there. I had heard about Francis and, though I hadn't yet caught a glimpse of him, I wasn't about to let him snatch a peek at me in the toilet.

Along the sidewalk, which led from house to outhouse, was a hedge of black raspberry bushes which supplied both families with many a tummy fill. A clothesline was strung along the sidewalks of both units. Not only did Mom hang the wash on the line, but she'd toss rugs over it then beat the dirt out of them with a wire heart-shaped rug beater. Always wanting to get in on that act Mom would turn the beater over to me. Beating rugs was a sure solution for releasing excess energy!

Each spring dandelion blossoms galore blanketed our lawn in a great yellow array inviting buzzing bumble bees and flighty yellow jackets in the warm sunshine. However, the bees hadn't bothered anyone in the shade beneath the apple tree. My sister and I plucked the blooms for our grandfather who paid us a penny a piece for each flower. Though it never amounted to many pennies before we grew tired of picking, Grandfather always managed enough blossoms to make dandelion wine from his favorite recipe.

Making further use of the dandelion in our yard, Mom brought out a sharp kitchen knife and the familiar dented pan which she used to peel potatoes. She'd pluck enough fresh green leaves for a big pot of Pennsylvania Dutch hot bacon dandelion gravy over greens and boiled potatoes. Mmm, we couldn't wait to eat it!

My dad's father, Mose, did not visit us all that often, however, one memory still haunts me. One day in our living room I was playing with a ball of clay. I had already assessed that my grandfather had a mean streak and was easily rattled, but I was as devilish at times as most pre-school kids. Tempted, I hurled the ball in his direction. My aim was reasonably good. I hit him right below the ear. As he turned toward me, I caught a glimpse of his neck. It was as red as a turkey gobbler. Boy, was he mad! I must've repressed all the words he hurtled back at me, but I recall they were not good. My sister watched the whole thing in disbelief. She never let me forget the incident either.

Centered between the two units of the house was a common water pump which had a workout every Monday—wash day. The two Graces took turns using the pump since, in those days, it was unthinkable to do the wash any other day but Monday. Mom kept the Easy wringer washer on the back porch in the summertime. Each wash day she rolled it into the kitchen. She filled a metal tub with water, heated it on the coal stove, then dumped it into the washer along with an unmeasured pouring of Super Suds. Each piece of laundry was tossed into the soapy water, then run through the wringer plopping into a tub of rinse water. Finally, the clothes were wrung through the wringer again. Mom loaded the rinsed laundry into a wicker clothes basket and hung the wash on the line to dry. It was a big chore for women in those days before indoor plumbing. I'm sure it must've been back-breaking.

The house exterior was yellow clapboard. Each side had a back porch divided by a pantry. In our kitchen stood a Kalamazoo stove with a top shelf on which Mom kept the Saltines. A black coal bucket with a chute claimed the left-hand side of the stove. A round rather crudely-cut hole in the ceiling above the stove allowed heat to enter the upstairs.

Mom kept tableware in the pantry cupboards along with glassware, canned goods, pots and pans, and "oil of gladness," a foul-tasting liquid vitamin. Mixed with a bit of sugar served on a spoon it helped make the medicine go down. Next to the Raleigh vitamin was a green tin of medicated ointment mostly used for skinned knees and elbows. A jar of Vicks vapor rub was handy for winter colds. At bedtime, Mom rubbed our chests with the camphor, eucalyptus, and the menthol scented ingredients, then covered it with flannel wraps. It was an unwritten rule that the rub is washed off before we could go out of the house the next day. Otherwise, it was thought, our cold cure might be hindered.

I remember finding tokens in the cupboard; wooden coin-like pieces in various colors. Mom said they were used to buy food during World War II days. Also kept in the pantry cupboard were the boxes of cereal: Shredded Wheat, Wheaties, Puffed Rice, Puffed Wheat, and All-Bran were the choices of the day.

15

Cheerios were introduced two months after my birth in May, 1941 as CheeriOats. We did not have candied cereal in those days. Supermarket choices were much simpler.

One day I managed to find a few tidbits of cereal on the cupboard shelf next to the boxes. After I'd about cleaned them all up, my sister shouted, "That isn't cereal. It's mouse turds!" Too late. I'd already swallowed them. I cringed at the thought of having eaten dried mouse droppings. Worse than that was having a younger sister know better than me.

In the pantry, Mom kept bread in a tin bread box. Often she made us toast for breakfast holding the bread with a fork held over the coal stove burner. Like the telephone, we did not have a toaster until 1950. Our first toaster was designed with two pull-out sides; a hand-me-down from Aunt Mary. Our first telephone was a two-line phone which we shared with the LeVan family. Two-line phones were still common through the 1960s.

Evenings when I was growing up without telephone or television we sat around the kitchen table creating flowers from colored crepe paper. Mom was good at making gladiolas; while my sister and I made bells. These were merely round cuts folded in half and twisted on a wire. Mom hung our bell flowers in a kitchen wall vase.

Other nights we'd gather in the living room. I loved when Mom read storybooks to us. My favorite was *Three Billy Goats Gruff*. Running a close second were Peter Pan books. I recall the first thing I ordered through the mail was something from a Peter Pan magazine ad. I was thrilled when my very first mail order arrived at the post office!

"Look! Look! Look! Look, Jane, Look! See Spot Run! Run! Run! Run!" Mom sat with me at the kitchen table while I learned to read the Dick and Jane books. Obviously, reading was taught by repetition as were the times tables in arithmetic class. To this day the sound of a car motoring in the distance reminds me of those days on Avenue E. The quiet of the evenings provided outdoor sounds that are unforgettable; a pleasant experience which is lacking today as the result of multiple electronic devices.

In the wintertime, after a day of playing "forts" in the snow and snowball throwing with the neighbor kids, the camaraderie continued in our respective kitchens as we knocked on the kitchen walls at night yelling out to each other. I have many fond memories of sledding on Shep's Hill on Avenue D; so named for the Shepperson family who lived at the top of the hill. On good snow days, the local police blocked the road off to motorists. Generations of kids were privileged to sleigh ride on Shep's Hill.

My mother's brother, Floyd, was our milkman. I can still hear the jingle of the bottles in the carrier growing louder as he approached our front porch. One day a week Mom paid him with pocket change. Delivery trucks in those days lacked heaters; thus it was a cold job in the wintertime. But he never came inside to warm up. He just trucked on until the day's deliveries were complete. His final stop was Dietrich's Dairy located near Peter's Ice Plant in Danville.

Sunday afternoons found my family sprawled on the living room carpet. *The Philadelphia Inquirer* and *The Bulletin* newspapers were scattered about the floor. I loved the funnies! My favorites were Little Lulu, Popeye, Mutt and Jeff, Nancy and Henry. I also admired the colorful Strawbridge & Clothier and John Wanamaker ads. Wistfully wondering what Philadelphia was like, I dreamed of owning the beautiful lacy dresses, frilly baby doll pajamas, and patent leather buckle shoes pictured in the papers. Even the lingerie was a sight to behold, yet the closest I came to such frilly underwear wasn't until the 1950s. "Days of the Week" panties in every color of the rainbow were a Christmas gift from Aunt Ann. Aunt Ann lived in the Philadelphia suburbs. I imagined that my panties were from Strawbridge and Clothier!

Our home was often warmed by music filling the air from our floor model Motorola radio. Songs and lyrics such as "Let's Go to Church," "Beyond the Sunset" and "Ivory Palaces" are three I most vividly recall. But even more memorable were the whistles, squeaks and static coming from that old brown box as we listened to *Baby Snooks*, *Fibber Magee and Molly*, and other old-time family radio shows. Later, in the 1950s, my sister and I listened to *Big Jon and Sparky* every Saturday morning. I can still hear the jovial chant as the show was introduced—"Today is Saturday, and there's no school today!"

During the winter months, Mom carried a bucket of coal from the cellar to the living room to keep our stove, a "bucket-a-day," burning. Our cellar was somewhat dank. I didn't go down there very often. However, in our cellarway was a cob-webby shelf where bottled root beer was kept. Dad, on occasion, made the root beer; then bottled and capped it with a bottle capper. It was fun to watch him store up this delicious treat.

Our living room furnishings consisted of 1940s furniture which included a round yellow faux leather hassock. It was perfect for turning on its side giving my sister and me rolls around the living room. We rode that thing until its seams burst and much of the straw stuffing had fallen out. It was in this room that my sister and I fought the measles, mumps, and chicken pox—the childhood illnesses in those days.

One of the earliest Christmases I remember, my sister had just recovered from whooping cough and was well enough to "go see Santa." Dad and Mom bundled us up in our woolen coats with mittens attached to strings running sleeve-to-sleeve. We wore matching leggings with the zippers running down the side seams. We were headed for the Riverside airport where Santa was to fly in from the North Pole. Excitedly, we watched him exit the plane throwing a big wave and a "ho-ho-ho" to the crowd. Everyone cheered as he climbed down the steps, toy-laden sack on his shoulder, and bumbled his way to the hangar building. There we waited in the long line of kids to give Santa our Christmas list which always included a doll. Jumping from his lap, we were handed a big orange and a giant coloring book, *'Twas the Night Before Christmas* by Clement C. Moore.

Dad had perched the Christmas tree in the corner of our living room. He had cut it from Bald Top mountain where his brother, Raym, and family lived on the "skunk farm." No, the tree did not smell like skunk and as far as I could tell there were never skunk sightings on the farm. The nickname had always escaped my understanding. Dad worked nights. I remember sitting in the living room with Mom on Christmas Eve. She instructed, "If you've been good, Santa will bring you toys but if you've been bad, he will leave you a bucket of coal." Uh-oh, I thought, as I ran the past year's events through my mind. But of course, I was a good girl and I envisioned a doll wearing a blue dress under the tree on Christmas Day. Sure enough! Santa did come with a doll wearing a pink dress for my sister, Linda, and a baby wearing a blue dress for me.

Dad had a sense of humor. He loved to hunt and fish. I don't know if it's true or not but Uncle David, with whom Dad often hunted and fished, shared this story: He and Dad were out on the river in their boat one day when a huge storm developed. Swift was the wind and, according to Uncle Dave, my dad took his coat off and held it up in the breeze blowing them back to shore. My Uncle Dave chuckled every time he told that story. I could only assume it to be true. It sounded like something Dad would do. But then, on second thought, it sounded a little fishy!

Dad was also creative. At Christmas time he'd gather princess and trailing pine from Uncle Raym's farm on Bald Top. He'd arrange the pine into wreaths and sell them to friends and family. He also kept one aside for his sister's grave at Odd Fellows Cemetery. Linda and I rode along to the cemetery whenever Dad was going to decorate her grave, but we were oblivious as to who was buried there. We had no idea it was our natural mother. We just played among the gravestones while he placed the wreath.

Dad worked for the Art and Bronze where iron was forged into ornamental railings. Reportedly, they can be spotted today in New Orleans. One time Dad brought home little cast iron piggy banks, assembled from two matching sides, for my sister and me.

In our living room one day I watched as Dad set up a gadget to which he attached fishing rods. He carefully turned the gear, while at the same time, winding vari-colored string around the rod. When he had finished one; it was quite the attraction. Dad had the gift, also, of building. I wish, as memorabilia, I still had the sandbox he built for my sister and me. It was square and attached to the box was a long seat on each side. Without a pattern, he designed a canvas roof to keep the sand dry when it rained. The canvas could be slid up and down the two side posts. I thought it to be rather inventive. Sadly, we didn't always get it down when it rained. I do not know whatever happened to it, but I'm sure it went the way of weathered and worn out toys.

Separated only by the wall between us, our home had steps leading to the second floor which ran alongside our neighbor's. There was a doorway from our living room that led to the stairway. One night we had visitors as was common in those days. Mom helped me into my flannel pajamas with the "trap door" in the rear. Even though we had company, Mom was getting me to bed. As she opened the door leading to the steps, I demanded, "You go first and I'll remain," lyrics from the song "Beyond the Sunset." No way was I going to let the boogie man catch me! As I lay in bed awaiting the sandman, the familiar sound of the night train clickety-clacking down the track, whistles blowing, lulled me to sleep. To this day I love that soulful sound.

Sometimes my dad's grandfather stayed at our house. I recall coming eye to eye with the buttons on Grampy's long johns. Poor old Grampy was switched family to family with my dad's brother on Bald Top. In the summertime, Grampy sat on his favorite chair in our yard smoking his pipe and watching us kids play. I loved my Grampy and I'm grateful Mom gave me his enamel dinner plate; saved for my grandchildren. He did not use a fork when he ate but preferred a knife. The sound of his knife sliding across the plate remains a pleasant memory.

Grampy was getting senile. One day we returned from town to discover he had cut down the cedar tree in our front yard. It was the twin to the cedar tree on the other side of the walk. I was very disappointed that our side of the house no longer matched the other side. Grampy had ruined it!

Around 1952, Grampy required nursing care. There weren't nursing homes in our area at that time so he was admitted to the "poor farm," the home in Montour County where those who couldn't afford healthcare lived out their final days. I clearly recall Dad taking me to see him at the home. Dad asked, "Do you know who this is?" Grampy said, "Yes, it's Kay." He died not long after that. While the barn has been torn down, the poor farm home has long been converted to offices. The red brick exterior remains as it had in the 1950s. When I pass by, I recall Grampy's window facing Sheetz, on Woodbine Lane.

It was around this time that Dad began inviting Bill to our house. Bill was a brother of one of Dad's second ward friends.

He was a single man who had mental issues; but not to the point that he couldn't be a trusted friend of our family. We welcomed him, and he came to our house often on his bicycle with a carrier seat. Though Mom was a little hesitant, I remember her letting me get a ride with him on his bike down Shep's Hill, the favorite sledding spot in the wintertime. Bill was quiet; an unassuming man whom I thought to be lonely.

In 1949, my dad was offered a little piece of land on D & H Avenue. Next to the railroad tracks, the lot was just a stone's throw from our house on Avenue E. Dad began to build our house making progress every chance he got. Mom, Linda, and I often walked from our house down to "the lot," as we referred to the site of our future home. Sometimes my grandfather Mose, an abusive alcoholic, would help. He and Dad never got along well; perhaps because both could be strong-willed. I was on the lot one day when they were constructing the house roof. Their arguing escalated into fiery darts and all manner of foul language. It caught my attention and, just in time, I looked up and saw my grandfather heave his hammer into the air. It landed with a thud against the roof.

Mom never favored alcohol which made an early impression on my life. One night Dad had gone to the fire hall with my uncle. Dad drank too much at the "hosey." He staggered into our living room and immediately began throwing up. I think my uncle escaped before Mom laid down the law. She demanded, "Don't you ever come home like this again in front of the girls!" Dad never came home like that again. Nor do I recall ever seeing beer in the refrigerator.

Mom came from a family of seven siblings. Their homestead was on Bald Top mountain, as was Uncle Raym's. Her siblings had sons, but daughters greatly outnumbered them. My sister and I had lots of girl cousins. We often got together as a family. Sunday afternoons back in the 1950s found us on the farm on

Bald Top. Friends and relatives gathered there. I can still see Grampy sitting in his chair, under the lanky maple tree puffing on his pipe, entertained by us kids.

The house on the skunk farm was somewhat primitive; having a dirt basement. The door leading from the cellar opened to a grape arbor. Jenny wren nested in that arbor year after year in those days. Down in the dell was a water well and pump that held a tin cup. We'd prime that well and wet our whistles whether we were thirsty or not; sharing the tin cup.

In my life, I had never shot a gun. My cousin, Butchy, wanted to teach me. We laid on the ground while Dad watched. He showed me how to rest the stock against my shoulder and, when I was ready, to pull the trigger. Bang! Off it went. My first reaction was the super loud blast right next to my ear; then the bucking I took on my shoulder. That one shooting lesson was enough for me. I still have an aversion to loud noises. Today I wouldn't know a bee from a bull about how to shoot a gun and I'm perfectly content with that.

I have many fond memories of those visits to Uncle Raym's place on Bald Top. I remember the juicy wild strawberries that grew in abundance on the hill not far from the house. Lingering still in my senses is the perfumed scent of pink trailing arbutus. Now extinct, or nearly, I wish I could get a whiff of it once again. I'm sure the aroma would carry me back to the former days on old Bald Top.

No longer can be seen from our former playground the sparkle of the Susquehanna River; nor the exquisite view of the steel bridge spanning from Danville to Riverside. The skunk farm location is no longer identifiable. The site has been replaced with a housing development mainly occupied by local professionals.

The Ace Cleaner school, Mesothelioma, and a Dangerous Species

We began the move into our new house in 1950. Since our rented place on Avenue E was not that far from the new home on D & H Avenue the move was fairly simple. Starting life in a new home meant that we had to leave behind many things we'd outgrown. I was now nine years old and had moved on to more pre-teen things. Gone was the sandbox Dad had built for my sister and me. We left behind the old wicker buggy. As kids, we ran that rickety thing around the tar-patched avenues of Riverside. On hot summer days, we removed our buckled sandals whenever we spotted water bubbles in the tar. It was much too tempting to pass up a bubble-bursting with our big toes.

We left behind our neighbors; the Kolenda family. However we had not left behind fond recollections of life on Avenue E. It was there I met my lifelong friend, Elizabeth, who taught me how to ride a two-wheeled bike. Somehow Mom appeared at the door that day. I can still see her beaming face as I passed by our house, Bitty trailing behind. It was there I learned to read Dick and Jane books around the kitchen table and how to create crepe paper flowers. It was there I learned how to be kind to those less fortunate as I watched Mrs. Johnson feed the bums. I discovered the taste of red currants and black raspberries right off the bush and how to prime an outdoor water pump.

Our new neighbors were Ed and Mrs. Stahl; as my sister and I referred to them. The Stahls had a grown son who was known as "Choog." I'm not certain why, but I suspect it was more a take-off on his name Charles than the fact that he lived by the railroad tracks. We had not known it at the time but, eventually, Ed and Mrs. Stahl would become the closest to being our grandparents that we had ever experienced. A sidewalk edged half of their house. Fascinating was a penny embedded in the cement which sparkled in the sunlight. Whenever I had occasion to walk past Choog's bedroom window I could hear music playing on his radio. I found it intriguing that he listened to classical music.

In their backyard grew feathery ferns and an overgrown wild cherry tree. In various shades of pink, it blossomed profusely each spring. In our neighborhood lived folks who had a son, Kent, a little older than myself. There were times he was forced to sleep in an outbuilding. Mrs. Stahl, as much as she could, took him under her wing and snuck food to him.

I was in fifth grade at the red brick elementary school on Gearhart Street. One day I observed Kent during recess. A shy and withdrawn boy, he stood in a corner back to the bricks. I had noticed the hole in the seat of his pants. He was not wearing underwear. I recall feeling very sad for him. Those days a child in a home such as his was simply swept under the rug. Kent lived a secret life. When grown, he served in the military and married a local girl. To this day I have not forgotten that recess when he must've been incredibly embarrassed.

On the other side of our home, the Bichners lived in their little white Cape Cod house. Catalpa trees grew next to their backyard garage. Referred to as "bean" trees, they were loaded with long seed-filled pods. Under the shade of the bean trees was a picnic table. On the corner lot, owned by the borough, grew a tall black cherry tree. In the summertime, my sister and I enjoyed many a munchin' on those delicious black cherries. Neighborhood boys climbed the trees and tossed them, on mini branches, down to us.

I guess Mr. Bichner had died rather young since there was never a dad around. But Eva remained in her home, sharing it with her son Dick. Dick was older than me and in high school in the early 1950s. One sunny day Mrs. Bichner entertained her lady relatives and friends. My mom, sister, and I were outside when all at once we heard a crash followed by roaring laughter. We looked over to see that too many ladies sat on one side of the picnic table. You can imagine what happened!! We joined the infectious merriment.

In the 1950s, moms always did spring and fall cleaning. One day Mrs. Bichner's sister was helping her with the spring cleaning. While I had never been inside the Bichner home, the room facing our house was obviously the living room. The ladies were in that room busily moving about. The curtains had been taken down; I supposed being washed. Linda and I were in Mom's bedroom when we caught sight of a mirror on their wall. I grabbed a hand mirror and we delighted in catching the sun's reflection in their mirror. Needless to say, their mirror didn't stay on the wall very long!

On the first day of May, my sister and I created little "May Day" baskets. We filled plastic containers with flowers we had

26

picked; then fashioned them with pipe cleaner handles. Off we'd go, running across the field to Mrs. Bichner's toting our surprise gifts. We delighted in hanging the baskets on her doorknob. We'd knock on the door, then run back across the field to home. We hadn't gotten to know Eva Bichner as well as Mrs. Stahl, but we knew how to be kind to our neighbors.

Mrs. Bichner loved the stemmy purple violets and the tiny attached love note. She had made a special trip across the field to tell our mother how happy it made her. She commented specifically on our excellent cursive writing skills. Thanks to the Palmer Method of handwriting taught in those days, my sister and I were both very good at it.

That first summer of the move into our new home Dad had constructed the cement porch cornerstones. Before the cement had fully dried, Dad suggested that my sister and I finger our initials with the date, "7/12/50," on the post of our choice. Today the impressions, though weathered, can still be seen. The true testimony to Dad's artistic talent, the sidewalk was laid with an elongated "S" shape. Dad was proud of the house he humbly referred to as "a little bungalow" whenever telling his friends about the house he had built for us.

Living by the railroad tracks, our address was North D & H Avenue, named for the Delaware and Hudson railroad. We enjoyed the luxury of indoor plumbing but had no bathroom; thus Dad built an outhouse in the backyard. Mom was now able to do her wash in the cemented basement where she had an automatic washer. On nice days she hung our clothes on the line outdoors; in bad weather the basement.

Behind the outhouse Dad had built was a plot where Mom and I carried the ashes from the furnace each winter. We lugged the heavy metal tub and dumped the ashes on the ground. I suppose today that would be considered an environmental hazard, but that's the way folks disposed of furnace ashes in those days.

We had a dinosaur of a coal furnace in the cellar. I watched as Dad wrapped the large duct pipes with asbestos. If I recall correctly, that required a wetting of the asbestos wrapping as he went. Dad carefully patted it down with his bare hands. Who had any idea, in those days, that asbestos would supposedly bear a connection to something called "mesothelioma?" I can't say I know of anyone who, in those days, contracted mesothelioma.

Directly across from our house was the railroad utility shed. Often I watched the workers ride the pump trolley up and down the tracks. My sister and I referred to it as "the paddy wagon." Directly across from the tool shed on South D & H Avenue stood Forney's coal yard; a coal dredging operation on the Susquehanna River.

On occasion in the summertime, Linda and I sat on the front porch eating apples and Saltines. We'd count the passing railroad cars using a telephone pole as a marker. Eagerly we waited for the caboose. We'd wave to the brakeman. He, enthusiastically, waved back. It felt like we almost knew him!

In the kitchen of our home, Dad installed what was called Congowall. It was a wall covering with a pattern of red and white squares. Our table was chrome with a Formica top. The chairs were chrome with red vinyl upholstery fashioned with bright silver brads. In front of the kitchen window was a red Cosco step stool. Linda and I always sat there when Mom washed us before bedtime using a basin of water, a washcloth, and towel.

Our refrigerator was a white icebox; a Frigidaire perhaps. I remember when we went grocery shopping at the A & P on

Ferry Street. My sister and I played at the Ferry Street Playground, across the street, while Mom and Dad shopped for groceries. Cole's Hardware presently occupies the property of the former playground. Last, we stopped at Peter's Ice Plant located on East Market Street, in front of Dietrich's Dairy. Dad pulled the car up to the dock, the iceman grabbed a block of ice with his tongs and dropped it onto our car bumper. In the summertime, we had to make the trip home quickly lest our block of ice melted into a snowball! Later, Mom and Dad purchased a refrigerator with a top freezer.

Our living room was furnished with a sectional couch and chairs upholstered in frieze fabric. Mom favored the new white wood furniture. Even our gossip bench matched the white coffee and end tables. We were not wealthy but, though I didn't know it, we had more than some families in those days.

Dad was overly strict, perhaps in part, because he felt a responsibility to our natural mother, his sister. We were not allowed to cross the railroad tracks and spent the first twelve years of our youth on the "upper" side of the tracks. The only time we were on the lower side was when Dad drove us that way in our Dodge. When I reached the eighth grade, there was a shortage of school buildings. Consequently, we were forced to attend school at a former clothes cleaning business. We referred to it as the "Ace Cleaner school." It was a small block building and, for the first time, we students experienced an indoor toilet. And, alas, I was able to cross the railroad tracks.

The school practically sat on the railroad bed. Thus when I was bored in the classroom, I'd watch the trains. As each colorful boxcar sped by the window, I'd dream of all the places that one day I might travel: Santa Fe, Bangor, Aroostook....

Three more memories stand out of those days at the Ace Cleaner school. Our classroom held both the seventh and the eighth graders. Penmanship was a required course and involved both grades. Our teacher, Mr. McCracken, made certain we had a flat eraser placed on the top of our wrists ensuring we kept our wrists flat on the desktop. Though penmanship was crafted with an ink-filled pen, on occasion we used a pencil. I had an aversion to the shaved edge of the pencil. It gave me the willies; thus I kept my fingers placed well above the edge. Mr. McCracken walked up and down the aisles to make sure each kid was going by the penmanship rules. I'd cringe when he came near my seat! I knew he was going to push my fingers down to the shaved edge of the pencil. He never knew why I kept them well above the lead.

During penmanship, Mr. McCracken played his beloved band music on the radio. I think we kids learned a genuine appreciation for band music rooted in the classroom in 1955. I'm certain many of us readily distinguish between a Glenn Miller hit and a Tommy Dorsey. To this day I treasure my tasseled Palmer Method Penmanship certificates of recognition.

One day in class we were learning the plurals of words. In those days the word "sex" was never a part of our vocabulary. However, I had been aware that it was in the English book. We were instructed, seat by seat, to quote aloud around the room. I counted down to "the word," and then counted the number of kids ahead of me. Sure enough! I was going to have to say "sex, sexes, sexes" out loud in front of the whole class. My heart raced as, finally, I spoke the words. I recall using perfect diction so that I wouldn't have to repeat the words. I wondered, at that moment, what the seventh graders thought since they had no way of knowing what was coming. Perhaps they weren't as timid as I. Certainly, they weren't as naive.

A third memory had taken place at Halloween. My friend, Clora, and I made a bad choice while at school one day. During that time of our lives, tick-tacking was simply throwing shelled corn on nearby porches after dark and then running. However, more serious and nasty was soaping windows. During recess, Clora and I plotted to soap windows that night. Of course, we could not pass up the Ace Cleaner school windows. The next day Mr. McCracken dismissed the class for recess. He instructed, "Now you may go out for recess and Clora and Kay will wash the windows!" How he ever found out it was us remains a mystery to this day. I can only guess he may have overheard our evening's plans or another kid reported us. Probably some teacher's pet! Whatever be the case, the windows we did wash…and boy, it was cold out! I may have been timid in the classroom, but when conniving with a friend I could become brazen! The Ace Cleaner building located on Avenue D, on or adjoining Merck property, has long been razed.

Riverside was never lacking in "mom and pop" grocery stores. Reminiscent of yesteryear's general store, Creasy's was no different. Across from the railroad station, Creasy's had a promenade-style porch and a screen door. Going there felt like some kind of magic! The same for the bubble gum machine just inside the door. In the eyes of a kid, the glass display counter seemed like a mile long. Better yet, it featured penny candy. I mean all kinds of penny candy! Candy buttons, wax "soda bottles" filled with sweet syrup, Boston baked beans, candy cigarettes, marshmallow ice cream cones and many more. My favorite was malted milk balls. Atop the counter were glass canister jars filled with more sweets: black licorice pipes, multi-colored jelly dots, and Mary Janes. It was always hard to choose five pieces. We kids lingered over the glass like boys picking out their favorite marbles.

Whenever we had a nickel we'd head up the street to buy a little brown paper sack of candy. I will always remember the creak of the screen door at Creasy's. Once inside you couldn't miss a certain smell. One would hardly find an oiled wooden floor as a pleasant odor but, to us kids, the scent meant candy heaven. Just inside the door to the right was the gumball machine. I'd exchange my nickel for five pennies and try for the lucky striped gum or a speckled one. The speckled one got you one extra free piece of candy, but a striped one netted you five pieces. For me, five malted milk balls! I can't say I recall another thing in Creasy's store though I'm sure it was every bit a grocery store.

In the l950s growing up in Riverside found folks outdoors always doing something. We didn't spend the majority of our day indoors as many do today. Children playing, moms talking over the fence, dads mowing grass were scenes of the day. Whirring motorboats cruising down the river and airplanes droning overhead were the sounds on Sunday afternoons. In the fall, the air was filled with the sweet pungent scent of burning leaves in neighborhood gutters. As I recall, in those days, no one complained of allergies. They seemed non-existent.

I loved the carefree days when I'd wash my long brown hair in the kitchen sink; then go outside to dry it in the warm sunshine. I recall one such afternoon in particular. Like most neighbors, my mom, sister and I were in the backyard. All at once the sky turned dark. Loud chatter began among the neighbors. Some were joking, "Is the world coming to an end?" It was awesome! After what seemed like a half hour, the blue sky broke through again. No one understood what had caused the darkness. Later, it was reported as smoke resulting from a fire in Canada. We never knew if that was the real source, but it made sense to us.

In 1956 I was in junior high school when our teacher asked us to tell a story about a time when we were really frightened. As I recall it wasn't Halloween, but thinking of a time when I was really scared wasn't hard for me. Speaking out in class wasn't something we did in those days so telling my story was, in itself, a frightening thought. But I mustered up the nerve.

I was in seventh grade and was just getting used to staying home alone at night. This particular evening Mom and Dad had run up to the neighborhood grocery store. We had no television and the radio was turned off. It was not "house noise" I heard, but it was clearly a bubbling sound.

I sat frozen until Mom and Dad walked through the door. Scared to death, I rattled off the noise I'd heard. They looked at each other; then Dad said, "Oh, it was just the wine bubbling in the cellar." I had been aware that Dad made, as a hobby, dandelion wine but I hadn't connected the noise with the wine.

Upon sharing my story the class broke into laughter! Now laughter wasn't exactly what I had anticipated. It was bad enough getting up the gumption to share my experience. I turned sheepish. Then one sharp boy shouted, "It's illegal to make wine!" Was I embarrassed! Not wanting Dad to get arrested or anything, I tried to explain it away. After all, Dad was not even a wine-bibber. As it turned out my scary story resulted in nothing more than a humiliating give-away; a tale I'll never forget.

It was during those early 1950s that rock and roll music had its birth. I most recall Kay Starr's "Wheel of Fortune" as the beginning of that era. Though it wasn't long before Bill Haley and the Comets came on the scene with "Rock Around the Clock." Many memorable songs preceded their hit. Songs like "Little Things Mean a Lot" by Kitty Kallen, "If I Give My Heart to You" by Denise Lor, and Johnny Ray's "The Little White Cloud That Cried." On occasion, I go to the Internet YouTube and lose myself in some of those old favorites. While listening to Santo and Johnny's "Sleep Walk," I'm back in high school. In the auditorium during lunchtime, the kids danced on the stage in white bobby socks. Or, I'm at the roller rink skating backward to Paul Anka's "Put Your Head on my Shoulder." Perez Prado's "Cherry Pink and Apple Blossom White" takes me to the Ace Cleaner school days. "Let Me Go Lover" by Joan Weber was another favorite when my generation experienced Dick Clark's first airing of *American Bandstand* in 1956.

At the Ace Cleaner school, we were permitted to play the radio during those cold winter recesses spent indoors. There were also days when the boys brought mercury to school and toyed with its beaded effects. No one ever thought that a day would come when mercury would be declared a "dangerous species!" No, no one ever died from the mercury we were exposed to before it was reported as a hazard to one's health.

The boys also created string tricks using their fingers and string. The girls loved playing games with the globe that hung on a pulley. We'd put our fingers on the world to "see where we traveled." There were always fun things to do in the days when hand-held gadgets were yet a future invention.

I was in eighth grade when Dad brought home our first television set. We were awed by this table-sized box with a round screen. I couldn't tell you if it was a Zenith, a Philco, or an Emerson. All I know is that when I got home from school I looked forward to watching such shows as *The Mouseketeers*, *The Life and Legend of Wyatt Earp*, and later in the evening, *The $64,000 Question*. When Dad got home from work, we'd eat supper around the table. Then, while smoking his Lucky Strike he'd suggest, "Let's watch Hopalong?"

Among other great black and white westerns were *Happy Trails* with Roy Rogers and Dale Evans, *Adventures of Wild Bill Hickok*, and *The Lone Ranger*. I loved sitting next to Dad, nibbling on oyster crackers, as we watched *The Cisco Kid*, a heroic Mexican caballero. We enjoyed watching *Gunsmoke* starring that handsome James Arness as Marshal Matt Dillon and his horse, Buck.

During those years of my mid-teens our local fire hall held movies on Friday nights. I recall being petrified after watching *20,000 Thousand Leagues Under the Sea.* Though it was merely a science fiction movie, a tour of the underworld, I found it frightening.

Chub Foust, a neighborhood friend, was instrumental at bringing about those old "fire hall movies." He was a barber who made house calls. My dad was one of his clients. One night my friend, Jan, phoned me. During our conversation, I mentioned that Chub was cutting Dad's hair. Jan said, "Ask him what movie will be on at the fire hall this week." Chub said, "The diarrhea sisters." I relayed that information to Jan. Then Mom said, "Nooo...." I had never heard the "back door trots" referred to as the diarrhea. My elders simply referred to it by its slang version! I felt like a fool when Mom explained the "technical" description.

Pennsylvania was an early riser among the drive-in movie theatre states. It was host to America's second drive-in movie theater which opened in April 1934. Shankweiler's, in Orefield—which is still in operation today—giving Pennsylvania the added distinction of being home to the oldest drive-in theater in America.

Oh what joy when the first drive-in theater opened on the highway between Northumberland and Danville. Our local outdoor theater was called the Arrow. There were times my sister and I went there with Mom and Dad. However, it wasn't until the teen years that I loved going there with my friends. Jan would round us up in her yellow Ford convertible and off we'd go to the drive-in. We bought our tickets at a booth just outside the speaker grounds. I recall a time when we hid a couple of kids on the back seat floor and covered them with blankets, sneaking them in for free. I think we did it more for the thrill of getting away with it than actually saving the cost of tickets.

After choosing a parking space, we hooked the speaker to a window. Rare it was to see a movie in the darkness in a car with the top down. We gabbed until the movies began. I have to tell you I cannot recall a single film I saw at the drive-in theater. There is, however, one memory of the drive-in theater that I will treasure forever. My husband gave me my engagement ring, in 1961, at a drive-in theater while waiting for the show to begin.

On occasion, the Arrow announced a "dusk to dawn" show. I'm not sure I know of anyone who didn't fall asleep during at least one of the movies featured at a dusk to dawn show. It was always good when one was not required to be at work the next day, as the night was long and sleep was scant. More often than not, we'd leave before dawn.

Drive-in movies were never short of food commercials on the big screen. When "Intermission" appeared, off we'd head for the concession stand for drinks, candy bars, and other treats. Mouthwatering ice cream was a favorite of old and young alike. The smooth flavor-rich delicacy was heaped to overflowing in a waffle cone. Delicious and refreshing, ice cream was always welcome on a hot evening at the drive-in. Popcorn, freshly popped and dripping with butter, was another crowd-pleaser.

We never had to concern ourselves with missing the beginning of a new movie while at the concession stand. I vividly recall the female voice announcing in measured melodious words, "The show is about to begin." At the end of a drive-in movie, we were instructed to "please replace the speaker on its rack when you're ready to leave. Failure to do so will damage both the speaker and your car. We'll be grateful and so will the patrons who follow you."

Saturdays in the 1950s found us at the local movie theater. Now defunct, ours was the Capitol Theater located on upper Mill

Street. Some of my fondest memories are of the old black and white westerns, the advent of 3-D movies, and the pre-show boring newscasts. My peers and I will attest to the fact that those were good old days in Danville. On Saturday afternoons a line of kids reached from the theater to the upper bank waiting for the doors to open. The Capitol Theater facade had an artfully-designed inlaid sidewalk similar to the Hollywood Boulevard "Walk of Fame." Centered was the round ticket booth.

During those years Saturday was the big day of the matinee! My friends and I exchanged thirteen cents for a ticket; then off we went into the darkness of the concession area. A flashlight-toting usher led us through one of the two entrances; half-wall sections with red velvet draperies matching those stretched across the stage. We'd chat over popcorn waiting for the show to begin. Finally, the curtains opened. The news was the first feature. I remember such reports covering Dwight D. Eisenhower "winning by a landslide" and much less boring news as Hawaii becoming a state.

My friends and I probably saw every notable movie produced in the 1950s. One I recall, *Ruby Gentry,* was filmed in the North Carolina foggy swamps. Starring Jennifer Jones as Ruby Gentry opposite Charlton Heston, I felt too young to be viewing such a sultry movie. But it didn't matter because I didn't understand it anyway. Films such as *Singin' in the Rain, Love is a Many-Splendored Thing, Shane,* and *Three Coins in the Fountain* were more my speed. While I never liked Jack Palance because he always played the bad guy, I especially liked *Shane* since I was near the age of Brandon deWilde. Then a baby-faced blonde, he died in a tragic car accident at the tender age of thirty.

Sometimes, in my younger years, Mom and Dad would take my sister and me to an evening show. We'd walk from Riverside across the old steel bridge with the wooden floorboards; then trudge back home after the show. I'll never forget *Song of the South*. There was standing room only that night in 1947. The theater had opened the curtains at the half wall dividing the seating area from the foyer. We kids sat on the wall; while the adults stood.

During that era, many people—mainly children—had been stricken with polio. Some of the news films depicted the afflicted suffering in iron lungs; assisted breathing machines. At intermission, a donation was taken for the March of Dimes— the organization targeting polio victims. During the offering, "Blue Tango" by Leroy Anderson was always played.

Oh, my first 3-D movie! I wore the green and red lensed disposable glasses and was set to watch *The Charge at Feather River*. I can even remember the section where I was seated when that Indian stood on the mountain and thrust that spear right into my face. I ducked and hit the back of the seat. Boy, that hurt! When the cowboys won, whoop-de-doo, I cheered!

Saturday mornings and "the races" were my favorites. Upon paying for our tickets, we were each presented a number from 1-10. Three-stooge-like characters rode bicycles, each with a number on his back. Comically, they went through various courses in their race for the win: falling into creeks, getting caught on tree branches, crashing, etc. In the end, all those who had the number of the winner received a free box of popcorn or maybe a Baby Ruth candy bar. Believe me, a whole lot of lively cheering went on during those races.

I remember the summer when there was a ringworm epidemic; a contagious skin disease which occurred on kids' scalps. The malady was short-lived; but you always knew which kids had it. Their heads were wrapped with white bandages. Nevertheless, that summer the ringworm epidemic did not keep us from walking over the bridge to Danville where ringworm was prevalent. Whenever I went to the movies Mom warned, "Now don't sit with your head against the seat!" My, I hadn't a clue as to how I would watch a movie sitting forward!

Today whenever a 1950s movie is featured on *Turner Classics* I can almost always say, "I saw that way back when." Somehow a televised replay is no match for those of the former days. When I hear "Blue Tango" I am reminded of the dimmed rainbow of colored lights. On each side wall, they were brightened for the March of Dimes offering. Indeed, visions of the iron lung are not quickly forgotten. Nor can I forget sitting on the wall watching Uncle Remus in *Song of the South*.

As I ponder those old movies, I recall Charleton Heston in the explosive scene of the chariot race in *Ben-Hur* and Philadelphia's own Grace Kelly starring opposite Gary Cooper in *High Noon*. To this day I can still hear the beat and the voice of Tex Ritter's "Do Not Forsake Me Oh My Darlin'."

Remembering those days I'd love to, once again, hear Mom yell "Now don't sit with your head against the seat!"

The Hell Hole

Bill, our many-years family friend, owned a blue Dodge a lot like the one Dad had purchased about l952. Bill often showed up at our house on Sunday afternoons after attending church. Mom always cooked a big meal on Sundays. We'd see his Dodge pull up in front of our house just about the time we were reading the Sunday papers, *The Philadelphia Inquirer* and *The Bulletin*. It was near meal time and we enjoyed having him with us around the table. After the nice dinner, Mom finished up the kitchen dishes. My job was to dry them.

It was Bill's habit, after a meal, to fall asleep sitting in one of the over-stuffed frieze chairs in our living room. When it came time for him to leave, as soon as he was out the door, my sister and I made a dive for his chair. Bill always dropped coins out of his pocket as he leaned into sleep mode. We couldn't wait to see how much change he'd left each time. Though it was fun, we always handed Mom the money. The following Sunday when Bill showed up Mom gave him the coins. "Bill you dropped your change in the chair." "Oh, did I?" as though it was the first time he'd done that. We could always anticipate another dash for his chair as soon as he'd leave.

Not only was Bill a perennial friend of the family, there were others over the years. Our house, like many homes in those days, had a "swinging door." We welcomed friends and family. In fact, one of those folks felt so at home that he helped himself to our refrigerator. We barely noticed. Mom was known for the good pies she baked and I'm sure her apple pie and a cup of coffee enhanced their visit to our home.

Bobby and Peggy McBride were family friends who visited often. One evening we were in the living room when Peggy played a little game with Linda. She held up cards from a deck; my sister would guess which card it was. Amazing we thought, she guessed every card correctly! Peggy was nonplussed. After they left I asked, "Lin, how were you doing that?" She said, "I could see the reflection in the window."

Some of Dad's old buddies from second ward often dropped in on Friday nights. Not only were they all hunting and fishing pals, but they loved watching boxing shows on the black and white screen. My sister and I learned that on Friday nights the television was theirs. That was the evening for the "Friday night fights." Madison Square Garden was the boxing mecca in the 1950s. I always got a chuckle watching Dad, crouching the edge of his chair, shouting at Jersey Joe Walcott or Rocky Marciano—"Give 'im an uppercut!"

Some days our cousin, Donny, came over with his second ward friends; Tucker, Ron, Dick, and others. We'd all sit outside in the cool of the evening those lazy, hazy days of summer. Front porch chatter was always a sweet time with the guys and our friends; Sally, Clora, Barb and other Riversiders. The fellows always wore black shoes shined to a hilt and hair greased in a "ducktail"—Elvis style. At that time Elvis had just hit the scene. One day my dad came home from work and said to Mom, "I saw Donny today. He has one of those Elvis Presley haircuts." I was surprised that Dad had even heard of Elvis let alone his hairstyle.

The first time Elvis appeared on *The Ed Sullivan Show*, he was shown only from the waist up. In those days, shock value wasn't the way singers behaved. Prior to the Elvis revolution, the closest anyone ever came to shock value was when Jerry Lee Lewis jumped up on the piano as he sang, "Whole Lotta Shakin' Goin' On."

In 1955 Elvis bought his first Cadillac, a pink 1954 Fleetwood Series 60. Elvis was known for wearing black, thus it became a fad for the teens of my generation to wear pink and black. It is interesting how a song places one in a particular place and moment which always evokes emotions. We fifties era folks occasionally share memories on Facebook, as well as songs on YouTube.

I suppose Dad learned to ice skate on the river in second ward where he grew up. It was winter 1958 when Dad took my sister and me to downtown Danville. We went into one of the stores where they sold ice skates. Linda and I tried on a pair and Dad bought them for us.

We drove, one night, to an ice rink in Milton. I learned, very quickly, the one big difference between a pair of roller skates and a pair of ice skates. When you bend over, you had to be careful to keep the blade from jabbing your behind. Since I was a good roller skater, I had no trouble flying around the ice on the first try. Then Dad joined me and I ice skated with my dad. It was the first and only time Dad had ever done a sport's thing with Linda and me. I treasure the memory of that moonlit evening. Who would have thought that my magical night of ice skating would prove to be the final highlight of bonding with my dad? Did I ever let the skates get out of my sight? No! I still have them among my souvenirs serving as a reminder of that special night, a star-studded evening to a seventeen-year-old girl.

Christmastime was always a happy time. However, in 1958 I was a senior in high school. That Christmas was anything but fun. I could not understand my dad's peculiar behavior. It all began when, for weeks following that November, Dad and Mom secluded themselves in the basement of our home. They were talking, rather fussing, for long periods of time. I never knew what the discussion was about, but I knew it had some driving force that caused my dad's irrational behavior. After some weeks, Dad no longer spent those hours in the cellar railing at Mom but his mental state worsened. Redfaced, he ranted in nonsensical outbursts. Just as quickly, he'd return to some state of normalcy.

Sometimes he spouted extreme foul language which, aside from cursing, I'd never heard come from his lips. As a seventeen-year-old, I didn't understand his craziness but I can tell you that our place was like a hell-hole. Weeks stretched into months and each week his mental state became more explosive.

One day Dad brought a bottle of acid home from work. He threatened to throw it in Mom's face. This went on for a time and we didn't sleep at night. People who lose their minds do not sleep, or so it seems. Night times became nightmares. In the darkness, Dad would circle our house. We never knew exactly where he was or what would happen next. Fear was a constant companion and Mom began to sleep with my sister. Needless to say, my grades fell my final year of high school.

For weeks Dad threatened to hang himself and, after a time, he had strung ropes in the cellar. He threatened to hang all of us. Those scenes run very vividly in my mind to this day. There were times when Dad would just up and leave his job. By this time he had been promoted to foreman where he worked on the shell line at Kennedy Van Saun. I can only guess he was able to escape his job long enough to taunt Mom.

One day I was walking on Walnut Street, I suppose to Geisinger where I worked part-time. I saw Dad's blue Dodge facing me in the distance at the traffic light. I knew it was him and that it was not time for him to be leaving work. Of course, he had seen me. As he passed by our eyes met but he made no motion nor did I. I do recall that I gave him a rather incriminating look and I could tell he caught it. As I write this, that moment is as real to me today as it was back then.

Another painful day Mom met me at the door as I got home from school. Her tone was desperate as she squalled, "Your daddy almost strangled me today. He had me down on the couch. I was able to get away and ran to Mrs. Stahl's." Most striking as I listened to Mom was the fact that, to the best of my knowledge, she had never been inside Mrs. Stahl's upstairs. Yet she had run directly for the only place she could think to hide. Dad had the cunning ability to turn off his red-faced insanity whenever someone outside of our family entered the picture. Thus, the episode ended at that point. I was devastated as Mom told me what had happened. First, because of what she had been through, but even more so because I was not there to help protect her.

Family members were aware of our situation, but they had no idea how hellish things really were at our house. They just said,

"Call if you need us." One time during a rampage I ran to Mrs. Stahl's to call Uncle Danny and Aunt Sarah. They came to the house, but Dad had turned things off. Thus, they left without incident. In those days, these were "things people didn't talk about" so my closest friends knew little of our situation. Certainly, no one in high school had any inkling.

One Sunday afternoon I finished work as did a friend. Mary Frances lived on our street. As we waited for her dad to pick us up, she questioned: "Why can't *your* dad pick us up?" I said simply, "He's sick." She quizzed me further, but knowing she'd never understand, I did not elaborate on Dad's insanity.

Somehow I had sensed that the answer to Dad's problem had something to do with God. But I didn't know much about Jesus, nor how to give Him to our family. One day I picked up our mail. It was not uncommon for us kids to read the mail as there was never anything personal about any of it. As I walked home from the post office, I read a letter that was addressed to Dad. I didn't know the writer, but he was talking about Jesus and I concluded that this might help my dad. When I got home I was eager to give it to him and said something like, "Here Dad, you should read this." But Dad scoffed and turned it away. I was deeply disappointed. We tried to think of various ways to get help for our family, but none of them were feasible. Even though I knew Dad hated him, I said to Mom, "Why don't we call Donny?"—our local policeman. But Mom said, "No, he'd kill him." And I knew she was right.

One day, while working on my job at the hospital, I had been in the dining room. I saw the brain surgeon in the line to get his lunch. I wanted in the worse way to speak with Dr. Hood but at age seventeen speaking with a doctor about one's personal life wasn't something you did. I let the chance go by.

One of the most difficult days during those long dark months was a Sunday afternoon when I had just gotten home from work at the hospital. Dad was sitting in the living room watching television. I went to the kitchen to wash my hands. Mom came alongside me and whispered, "Your daddy put Bill out today." I was shocked. I asked, "What happened?" She said that when Bill came to the door, Dad sent him away and told him not to come back again. I asked, "What did Bill do?" She said he asked, "Why Chub, what did I do?" I was deeply crushed knowing how much we meant to Bill all those years and I knew a part of his life had been taken away.

There were times over the ensuing years I'd be walking on some street in Danville and I'd spot Bill across the street. For whatever reason, he always walked with his head held upward gazing straight ahead. It was simply his normal stance. I knew he had not seen me; so I left it at that and did not call out to him. Each time I saw him I was reminded of that day Dad put him out. I felt compassion for him. His loss was our loss too.

Today whenever I go past his former home at 123 Wall Street I am reminded of the former days. His house is easily remembered because I mailed out the family Christmas cards each year. Bill has been gone now many years, but I have fond memories of his visits to our house when I was young, even into my teen years.

Aunt Mary and Uncle David were always a part of our lives. They had lived directly across the river; their house visible from our house. One day Aunt Mary visited as was her daily habit. It always seemed that Dad could hold out only a short time before the pressure burst. Aunt Mary left but watched through a window. She witnessed, from our porch, my dad's dam of emotions erupt. Though she never doubted our claims about Dad's craziness, she now saw it for real. The following day she came over and emphatically stated, "When I left last night I watched from the window and I saw everything." Somehow I felt relieved that at least someone else had seen Dad's abusive behavior as it played out.

Though I don't know how he did it, Uncle David succeeded in getting Dad to Dr. Curry's office. But as soon as the doctor began to press on his stomach in the routine examination, Dad jumped from the table and ran outside. That ended any chance for a physician's evaluation.

There were no answers.

Dad continued to warn us he would hang himself. One day he approached me in the living room. "Kay, the car's yours," he said. I can't tell you what I thought at that moment, but it certainly wasn't an eagerness to have a car.

Sometime after the fact, my cousin told me that one day during a time when Dad was at their house they were watching television. I suppose it might have been a western. Ellen said an actor in the movie hung himself. Dad said, "That's how I'm going to die." It was chilling!

Sunday night, April 5, 1959, I returned from the roller skating rink. As soon as I got in the door, I knew things were bad. In fear, I remember standing on the heat register. Inwardly I was shivering with fear. Seeking warmth and security, I suddenly remembered it's April, the heat isn't on.

The following morning was a bright and beautiful sunny day. My sister and I were in bed as it wasn't yet time for us to get ready for school. Forever etched in my mind are Mom's cries as she climbed the steps from the cellar. "He hung himself in the cellar. He hung himself in the cellar." I was on my feet before I was awake. I will never forget that moment. Her wails and sound of her steps as she ran up from the cellar haunt me to this day.

In some sort of huddle, we all screamed as Mom yelled, "Call Mary!" I quickly phoned Aunt Mary and Uncle Dave. I can tell you that amid the screaming a relief swept over me that felt like the most gigantic black cloud one could ever know had lifted. The first thing my aunt asked, "Was it just him?" I said, "Yes." Even over the phone, I sensed her enormous relief. They were at our door in what seemed like a mere five minutes. That day I opened *The Morning News* to read the obituaries. Dad's read: "Joseph F. Stetler, 41, Riverside."

We were late getting to the funeral home the night of the viewing. I remember Mom let us wear our short furry white coats she had gotten us for Easter. She worried that they were white and, in those days, it was common to wear black. But it wasn't as though we knew when we'd need a black coat. Besides, I loved my white coat so no matter. As we pulled into a parking space on Ferry Street I saw a group of my high school classmates leaving the funeral home. I was relieved that I didn't have to face them under the circumstances. They couldn't know what our lives had been like those final days of my high school years. Suicide brings such shame. Since no one knows the circumstances, too often they draw their own conclusions. It happened in our lives, but we never let it get to us because we knew the story from the beginning to the end and there was never anything for which it was necessary to feel any guilt.

I have a clear memory of the funeral parlor as the preacher, Reverend Flowers, gave a message the following day at Dad's service. I remember his words, "Ashes to ashes and dust to dust," though I understood little about death. Deep in my soul, as I listened to the minister, I wondered about life after death. I had also been keenly aware that the bondage of Dad's overly-strict parenting had ended. I felt a new sense of freedom which I had not known until those moments after Dad's death. Yet I had no plans to rebel against my mom. My sister and I had never given Mom and Dad any trouble and a thought of changing that was never a part of my thinking. Now there were three of us. I knew we had to make the best of it. In the days that followed Dad's burial, Mom never stopped weeping. In fact, for some days following the funeral, she wept every morning as soon as she awakened and realized....

Although Mom had never worked outside the home, she enjoyed housecleaning. She made the decision to apply for a job in the housekeeping department at Geisinger. She was readily hired. I regretted that she had to go to work, but I was happy that she would be employed where I worked.

We left home after Dad's suicide and lived for several months, across from the present Dunkin Donut, with Uncle David and Aunt Mary. It was very hard to know that Mom would eventually have to face the cellar again; and so would my sister and I. Since Uncle David had taught me to drive, I now was licensed and "the car was mine." On occasion, I'd drive Mom and my sister over to the house to check on things. We had missed summer at home and now autumn had settled in and leaves were falling to the ground. The rooms on the second floor above my aunt and uncle became available and we had rented that part of the upstairs.

Our apartment was adjacent to a bar which had an unkempt garbage area. Mom had kept a bowl of potato chips on the kitchen table and we became aware that something was eating them. There were also other tell-tale signs that a rodent had gotten into our apartment though we could find no hole. Then Mom moved the curtain aside. It seems that a rat had found its way through a hole underneath a kitchen curtain. In the night we could hear it thudding around and, even though it was only a rodent, we didn't need a rat at that time in our lives. We had left the bedroom to sleep in the living room which had a door we could close. Our lives had once again been driven by fears. Then one day without a hint Mom said, "Should we go back home?" My sister and I said, "Yes!" We had spent Christmas in the apartment and now winter had passed. As we pulled into the driveway at our house it felt like heaven. The trees had leafed and everything seemed so beautiful. We were back home. Mrs. Stahl came out to greet us. "Oh Grace, I'm so glad you've come home." Her words were a healing balm. It was one of the happiest days of my life. And I know now that God had sent us a rat! He had used a rodent to buoy us on to moving back home.

As we settled in, I knew we had to face going down to the cellar. In the past, as my sister and I were growing up, my mom always gave us our Saturday morning bath in the cellarway. Now we had to face the cellarway again but in a different way. We did so without ever saying a word. Sometimes in life, there are things we must do whether we like it or not. And that is how we approached facing the cellar again.

Somehow Mom made sure we had a Christmas tree that year when Dad was no longer around to do it. I'd lined the front door window with paper doilies and Christmas cards we'd received from past years. By now most of my closest friends had married, but Jeannie remained single. She and I had gone shopping in downtown Danville. I noted that she liked a particular pocketbook in J. J. Newberry's. I told Mom about it and she said, "Get it, and we'll wrap it up and put it under the tree for her." What a delight it was to see her eyes light up as she tore open the bright red wrapping on Christmas Day!

All my growing up years, Mom was both protective and supportive. Dad was our provider, but Mom was the one who encouraged Dad, "You have to let them go sometime." Growing up, I had not understood Dad's fears for our safety. They might have been rooted in those events surrounding my early life when I lived with my grandparents. That would make sense. In fact, those events may very well have been the seeds for Dad's mental state later in his life.

I recall one day when he was having his after-dinner cigarette. As always, he was still sitting in the kitchen chair. I was in the living room. I looked up at him. He was looking at me with tears in his eyes. I sensed what he was thinking, but said nothing.

Earlier, when I was about eight or ten years old, a woman who lived across the railroad tracks from our home had told Clora and Jeannie a secret about my sister and me. They could not keep it to themselves. There, in an orchard field is when and how I learned that my sister and I had been adopted. From that time, I had determined if Mom and Dad didn't want me to know I would seal that secret in my heart.

Over the years, on occasion, we'd bump into folks who knew the story. Subsequently, they broached the subject. Mom always looked at me and said, "Kay go see if...." There was always a way she maintained protection from the tragic events that had taken place in 1943 behind Shooters Bar. Promising myself I would never let my own secret slip out of the envelope of my heart, I'd go obediently. Once, when I returned to the adults, I heard Mom trailing off the conversation, "No, they don't know anything about it."

One Saturday Aunt Mary was at our house. She and Mom were chatting in the kitchen. I was in bed yet, but awake, my bed facing the open hallway. Then I heard Mary say, "Grace I think Kay knows." Mom said, "Oh no. She doesn't know anything about it." Then Mom popped her head into the hall to make sure I was asleep. Of course, I was asleep.

51

The Roller Skating Years

My first skating experiences were that of wearing "clamp-on" roller skates, which required a key to fasten them to our shoes. My sister and I both had a pair. Keys were easily lost but, when we were lucky to have a key, we could make them work on our sandal shoes. We learned to roller skate on Mrs. Stahl's sidewalk. We had to use the key often as those old roller skates didn't stay well on shoes of any kind. Later when we heard the old, then defunct, roller skating rink was going to open we were delighted. The rink, only a few blocks from our home, had a nice wooden floor and all the boarded windows opened upward enabling a three-sided exterior view in the summertime. We readily learned how to do the "two-step," which was a skate dance back in the fifties. Everyone skated the two-step and we became good at skating backward. Most of the time we dressed up in full skirts, believe it or not, and rarely fell.

I do remember one girl bending her knees on her skates catching her skirt as she rolled forward. It was the only time I ever recall an "accident" on the skating rink floor while wearing a skirt. I was glad it wasn't me!

Janet my friend, and I, along with a couple of other girls became regulars kind of like the *American Bandstand* teens. We got to know the manager, Paul, very well both as a friend and rink supervisor. One day Paul asked my friends and me if we would like to become "skate girls." There were also "skate boys." They were the fellows near our age who swept the rink floor before a skate time. They helped skaters up from the floor when they had fallen and adjusted skate wheels, etc. We agreed to be skate girls. We didn't know it at first, but that meant we didn't have to pay at the ticket booth for admission. Tickets back then were fifty cents, but we needed only a dime for a soda and fifteen cents for a bag of potato chips for skate time. Our job was to teach beginners how to skate; though those times were rare.

As skate girls, we enjoyed free skating all of our teen years. We, too, went to skating rinks in other towns. Sometimes we'd pool some change together for gas which, at the time, was twenty-nine cents a gallon. I remember one occasion asking the gas attendant for sixty-eight cents worth of gas. It was enough to get us to Dixie's Starlight Gardens in Bloomsburg; then back to Danville. In those days we went roller skating five times a week and worked part-time jobs at the hospital.

I remember many of the skate styles of the day. "Trio Kentucky Steal" was my favorite. A trio skated together around the floor; when Paul blew a whistle the two on the outside moved ahead to the next person in front of them. Sometimes it was boys' trio, other times it was girls' trio. We also did the "Whip," which needs little explanation. We just simply joined hands and snaked around on the rink floor, the leader making as many attempts as possible to "crack the whip." You didn't want to be the last person on the string since that one had the furious whips!

On New Year's Eve, we had a blast at the rink. At midnight Paul served everyone hot dogs and sauerkraut on a bun. It was always good clean fun and we kids never had time for alcohol; nor had we ever given thought to drinking parties. As good skaters, my friends and I were nearly always privileged to have a guy ask us to skate on "men's choice." On "lady's choice," we girls had the chance to choose a guy. I loved those "Moonlight Couples" when the rink lights were dimmed; the stars on the overhead crystal ball reflected on the floor. Our favorite romantic songs were played: "Only You" or "My Prayer" by the Platters, "Love Me Tender" by Elvis, "Devoted to You" by the Everly Brothers or "The Twelfth of Never" by Johnny Mathis. It was with sadness when the night had ended with a Moonlight Couple, the last song played—"Goodnight Sweetheart, Goodnight" by the Spaniels. Little did we realize then, that one night would be our last to skate to that song as we moved on toward adulthood and marriage and our skating rink days were over. On occasion, I recall those fun times with a tugging at my heart to do them all over again.

It had been several years since we'd seen Paul. My friends and I were attending the Bloomsburg Fair. As we walked around the fairground, there ahead of us, we spotted Paul! We were all so happy to see him again; but a bit taken aback that he used a wheelchair. The last time we had seen him he was wheeling on his skates. He was happy to see us again. I do not recall anything of our conversation except for one thing; he spoke about Jesus. Somehow, I suspected, our old friend had "gotten religion." I hold out hope that I will see him again one day when I reach heaven's shore. Perhaps he will be serving hot dogs topped with sauerkraut!

Better to have Loved and Lost

From my earliest years in Riverside, I had friends. As a preschooler, I first met Mary Kay, then later "Bitty." Elizabeth was a year older than me. She lived up the street and was, at that time, my closest friend. We did many things together over the years and I treasure those memories; one of which was the day we dug a big hole in her backyard. We spread some plastic over the hole and then filled it with water. Next, we added Kool-Aid for color. To our dismay, the water immediately seeped out. So much for our backyard swimming pool.

Mary Kay and I began first grade in 1947. Later, Lois and Janet attended our Riverside class. We were friends all through high school; then went our separate ways as those three had married. But Jeannie remained unmarried. Jeannie and I had gone roller skating Sunday night Christmas week, 1959. By then I was eighteen and had gained a little weight.

Sometime during a round on the skating rink floor, I saw a couple of boys enter the rink. I was surprised to see it was Bill and Jim; brothers I had known from high school. They were now in the military. I could tell I had caught their eye. My change from skinny to "just right" improved my self-esteem and I enjoyed their attention.

Secretly, I had hoped to get a phone call from one of them that week and, the next day, I did. It was Bill, and I said "yes" when he asked me out. I must've squealed in delight after hanging up the phone. I didn't, but I was "over the moon" before anyone ever landed there! I'd always been thin and didn't rate with the boys, therefore dating was new to me. All week I practiced introducing Bill to my mom. "Mom this is Bill." "Bill, I'd like you to meet my mom." I was both excited and nervous when he arrived at our place that Saturday night. In truth, I did not know how to act. My biggest fear was making a big blunder or worse several blunders. I was not accustomed to a boy opening the car door for me but, when we approached the car, I managed to get through that without a stumble.

He drove me to Berwick where the movie *Peyton Place* was showing. As we crossed the street to the theater, I felt about ten feet tall walking next to this man in military gear. The theater was packed. Then I made my first blunder! Somewhere in the movie one of the actors asked, "Have you ever went swimming in the raw?" Everyone laughed. Except me. In fact, not only had I never heard the phrase "swimming in the raw," in my life I'd never even been swimming. That was one of those things Dad didn't let my sister and me do for fear of something happening to us. Then I asked, "What does that mean?" Bill, somewhat embarrassed as well, awkwardly waved his arm and said, "It means swimming without any clothes on." I thought I'd die! I felt stupid in my ignorance and worse was feeling I was the only one in the theater who hadn't laughed.

Driving home from the movie, Bill stopped at a restaurant as most dates had back then. I froze. I wondered, how am I going to eat anything in front of this handsome guy? I rarely ate, to begin with, but to eat in front of a boy? I couldn't do it! The waitress gave us ample time to decide on what we wanted to eat. When she approached our table to take our order, I sheepishly said, "I just want a Coke." Being the gentleman he was, he too, ordered a Coke. I have a faint recollection of clinking my glass against my teeth at first sip! Adding to the chill was that we were the only diners in the room. By then I pretty much knew I'd blown the whole date. I was right. I didn't hear from him again. How could I have been so stupid? I lamented for days. I couldn't help myself.

Soon after my bungled date, I drove past their house. I spotted Jim in the yard and pulled over to speak with him. From the outset, I was comfortable with him. He was very different from his brother and, in short order, we were dating. He continued to show up at my house in his parents' red and white late fifties Chevy. After a time, we were "going together."

Jim was stationed in another state. Nearly every weekend he thumbed a ride home to Danville. Our relationship grew. However, hanging over my head was knowing he faced an eight-month military voyage. By then I was in love for the first time. Cruising around in the fifties was the thing to do. Thus we drove around the various local towns. Then, Sundays at sunset, he began the long trek back to his base.

As I best recall, it was on my birthday that he had given me a gold bracelet with jet black oval-shaped gemstones. Though I have not worn it since those days, I still have the bracelet.

Soon the day came when he had to leave for the cruise. By then, it was assumed that we would get married when he returned. At least that was the implication. Days turned into weeks and weeks turned into months. We wrote letters all the while. His, on Navy stationery with his ship logo, mine on parchment paper. In one letter I recall him telling me about a beautiful sunset he'd enjoyed; writing that it was "a picture no artist could ever paint." Another time he wrote, "If I encounter a girl I tell her 'got senorita back home.'"

My friend, Lois, and I had our pictures taken at Muzzy Studio in downtown Danville that summer. The storefront, years later, became my Christian bookstore. I couldn't wait to send Jim my new 8 x 10 black and white photo. I had wallet sized ones made to send to girl pen pals with whom I'd written from my earliest teens.

That summer Mom may have wanted to spare me any unforeseen change of heart. She reminded me more than once, "Kay, what if he comes home and doesn't want you?" I always brushed it off. Not in a million years, I thought. We were getting married. I'd treasured the shoebox which held dozens of his letters. That summer my friends and I went to the skating rink, the movies, and a day trip to the Gettysburg Battleground. I never looked at another guy.

Jim was to have returned sometime at the beginning of October. There was no clear indication of an arrival date. At the same time, I wondered why he wasn't providing more precise information. Then, I noticed the letters were dwindling. However, I repressed my concern.

At the beginning of that month, I was working a full shift on the weekend. It was a late Sunday afternoon and I was driving home. I stopped at a red light at the corner of the upper bank on Mill Street. Then, I saw it! The red and white Chevy. I first noticed as I waited for the green light that Bill was driving. Then I looked to the other side. My heart sank. There in the passenger's seat was Jim! I saw him rest his head on the back of the seat feigning sleep. I suspected his brother had seen me and alerted him. His pretense, in my mind's eye, was as though I would think he'd had a long journey home.

I was stunned and heartsick. Not only did he not arrange to meet me on his arrival home but he'd tried to hide from me. I drove home and related the incident to Mom. That night, he did come by the house. I thought everything was still going as planned in nearly every letter I had received from him. He then indicated that he would come to pick me up the following morning. I couldn't wait!

Mom had gone to work. My sister was home, but I'd hardly noticed. I bathed and dressed in something I thought was very special. Then I waited and waited. An hour or so had passed and I kept checking the front of our yard for his car. As time passed, Mom's words kept haunting me. What if he comes home and doesn't want you? No, I couldn't accept that. Hours passed. I was forced to come to grips with her warning. Perhaps she was right all along. How could this be? I had all his letters, the most recent of which he "couldn't wait to see me." Or, had I just read more into his words?

Mom came home. I dreaded the fact that I was still there and hadn't been with him. I didn't even have to tell her. I said, "He never showed up." Mom, though I know she hurt too, said, "I told you. I was afraid all along...." Her demeanor was reassuring rather than harsh. How was it Mom could somehow have an intuition that had entirely escaped me? Love is, indeed, blind. The ensuing days were a blur. Often I wept, even at work sometimes, though I managed to do my job and somehow make it home each day. I still watched the front yard, hoping I'd look out and see the red and white Chevy, but it never happened.

Weekends I'd drive by his house on my way to work. I was always eager to see if he had come home for the weekend.

59

Sometimes, against my own rules of letting the guy take the lead in a relationship, I'd break down and phone him. Nearly always one of his sisters answered the phone and, of course, he "wasn't there." For weeks, then months, I'd keep an eye to see if he had come home that weekend. My heart died on Sundays as the sun set, knowing he'd once again return to his base without so much as a phone call.

My friend, Jeannie, kept me going. One time we'd stopped at our usual pizza place. Barbara, our waitress, asked, "What's wrong with you…you haven't been yourself?" I must've mumbled some response, though I do not recall it. Adding to my pain was the deep sense of loss of my dad to suicide. I was deeply depressed. It had taken a year before my heart had healed enough to move forward.

When we go through deep sorrows and great tragedies in life, the pain may be forgotten, but the scars always remain. It is through our heartaches and our struggles that we are strengthened in both body and soul. We come out of the burning ashes having been molded into the person God wants us to be. Whenever I look back on the tragedies of my lifetime, I am reminded that Jesus wants to use us to help others when they go through great troubles and deep water. Indeed, the best counselors are those who have been through the fire. No one else can more effectively understand another's pain.

Little could I have known that someone was waiting in the wings for a chance to see me. I had met Lawrence several years before, in passing, through a friend. All I knew about him was that he drove fancy cars! Though I was not that impressed with flashy cars, his was probably either an Oldsmobile or a DeSoto. That's how much, or should I say how little, I knew about cars. While I was getting to know Lawrence, we cruised around town in his big-finned vehicle always with the radio on. Songs I loved were "Are You Lonesome Tonight," by Elvis

Presley, "Last Date" by Floyd Cramer, and "There's a Summer Place," by Percy Faith. Whenever I heard one of those songs the pain of having lost my first love burned deeply in my heart and I floated into flashbacks which my mind wouldn't let me escape.

I still grappled with the question, "Why?" While I had gotten past the critical early stages of the loss, I found it difficult to find closure. Prolonging my grief was my search for the reason Jim had changed his mind. Had we been intimate, I might have had some understanding, but we hadn't been. Months had passed, and I was too proud to ever approach him and ask "Why?"

Lawrence and I grew to know each other. But I struggled to find my place in our relationship. I had just wanted to run. Still deeply depressed, I wasn't sure what I wanted. It had seemed that everywhere I went Lawrence would show up. I had gone to Knoebels roller skating one Sunday night. While rounding one of the turns on the skating rink floor I looked up. There he was peering through the screened window.

In July of that year, I had a chance to go with my friend, Karen, to Brigantine, New Jersey. Karen and I had agreed to go on the week's trip with her sister, Nancy, and her family. She and Dick had rented an oceanfront cottage. We had agreed that, in exchange for the week at the shore, we would babysit the children part of the time. Except for the huge biting horse flies that were apparently drawn to water we enjoyed the beach. Karen and I kept our promise to watch the children while her sister and Dick enjoyed a night out. We loved hearing them share with us their evening's events and how they had met several couples. We were glad our babysitting had allowed them to have a good time away from the children.

Toward the end of the vacation, Karen and I were walking from the cottage to the frontage of the beach. I had been looking elsewhere, but Karen had been looking straight ahead. All at once she whispered, "Kay! Guess who!" Yes, it was Lawrence in his new white Chrysler Newport. I couldn't even go to New Jersey without him trailing me! Admittedly, I held to a deep commitment that a guy ought to pursue a girl rather than the other way around. Secretly, I loved it!

That summer I wavered from happy moments to deep regret. The shocking suicide of my dad followed too closely by the loss of my first love. I was overwhelmed. Lawrence wanted to marry me, but I honestly didn't know what I wanted. He treated me well and gave me nice gifts. One night he had given me a lovely jewelry box which, when opened, a ballerina twirled to "Let Me Call You Sweetheart." Although the music no longer plays, I still have the jewelry box among my souvenirs. Another time he had given me a beautiful opal-studded bracelet. When I got home that night, I showed it to Mom. She said, "Kay, he treats you well," an unspoken indication that he would be a good husband.

Lawrence had lived on a farm. He was an only child and had graduated from high school just two years ahead of me. We had much to which we could relate since we'd both attended Danville High School. I had come to respect him as a hard worker. He had earned every big-finned car he'd ever owned. My mom and dad had always been true to their word as well as true to each other. Mom always said, "You make your bed; you lie in it." I'd heard that instruction many times in my teen years. Thus I struggled with what I really wanted. Lawrence and I had taken a day trip to Gettysburg that summer to tour the battleground. I had taken many photos with my black and white Brownie Hawkeye camera. On the drive back to Danville we had stopped at Angie's Diner; a popular restaurant north of Harrisburg. It was a memorable day.

All the while I worked full time at our local hospital. After work, I gave Rosie a ride home. Rosemarie and I opted to work in the dietary office after graduation from high school. As we wrote patients' diets, we'd talk about our boyfriends. I remember Rosie's counsel, "No use washing and ironing for someone you don't love." I felt torn into pieces that summer. Finally, I told Lawrence, "Okay, I will marry you if you promise me one thing…that you won't move me to the farm." After living in town all my life, I could not come to grips with living in the country. I had been well aware that he had started out as a young teen hauling milk in cans for his dad's business. Yet, I could not imagine life on a farm after living in Riverside.

While waiting for dusk and the movie to begin at a drive-in theater, he gave me my diamond ring. When I got home that night, I couldn't wait to show it to Mom. She was happy for me, and I was committed to my future wedding plans and my marriage.

We married at my hometown church, St. Peter's United Methodist Church, in Riverside where I'd spent many happy times growing up. There was Sunday school, Girl Scouts, classes every time the Ace Cleaner school furnace malfunctioned, Christmas plays, and many other events. That day, Saturday, September 30, 1961 was lovely and seemed more like the middle of June. After opening all our gifts at our church basement wedding reception, we left for a honeymoon trip to Niagara Falls. Like many others in those days, I'd never experienced traveling. When we reached the bridge crossing into the Canadian side, I heard the roar of the falls. I was astounded. Finally reaching the Horseshoe falls at night time, the sight was impressive! Multicolored lights enhanced the glitz and glamour. Niagara Falls was, indeed, a welcoming spectacle. Preferring to do our own thing, we opted out of expensive tours. Words can hardly describe the beauty of the most famous falls in the nation. We also toured the American side of the falls, including the Bridal Veil Falls. We stayed at the Honeymoon Motel. Later, we rented a room at Morean's Motel and ate breakfast at their cafe. Little had I realized, at that time, that one day I would visit Morean's Motel as a widow. Once again I ate in the little cafe while on a traveling sales position for a Christian distributor.

When the week ended we headed back to our rented apartment in Danville to begin our lives as husband and wife. Our living quarters had a cute little kitchen, tiny bathroom, living room and a small bedroom. Our pink Princess telephone did not have a bell, but rather the sweet sound of chimes.

At Christmas time I decorated the living room in the many crafty ways I had trimmed our home when I was a teenager. I remember using mirrors to double the beauty of the Christmas tree and colorful lights. That December I invited my co-workers from the office for a little Christmas party and gift exchange. I loved entertaining and was happy to share our new first home with my gal friends over cake and ice cream.

In those days it was not necessary, when renting an apartment, for a lease. People were honest; leasing contracts were unnecessary. Rent was paid with cash and you received a paper receipt. Unlike today, it was common to move out with little notice as rentals were in demand.

While it had been totally unthinkable for me to move to the farm, the following February Lawrence's parents offered us a small plot on which, if we wished, we could set up a mobile home. We did shop around for a mobile home. The homes we looked at were awesome! After driving to several nearby towns, we finally settled on one we loved—a New Moon. It had a light green and white exterior and two "expandos" which, when opened, gave the exterior of the home a T-shape. The "T" was our living room. The home was equipped with a lot of jalousie windows. They were really nice as we could leave them open in the summertime and not be concerned about rain should a storm develop while we were away.

All of our appliances were pink! A pink washer enclosed in the kitchen, a pink refrigerator, a pink sink, a pink gas stove, a pink bathroom bowl and a pink bathtub! I loved it and my husband liked anything that pleased me. Now Lawrence was close to his work on the farm. I had to drive the five-mile trip to Danville for work, but I was okay with that once I learned how to get back home.

I had three different choices of roads to travel. In the wintertime driving down "frog holla" was my favorite. It was lined with colossal pine trees. Whenever it snowed the drive was a winter wonderland. Several years later the road had been widened. Sadly all the big pines had been sacrificed. Even worse, they were left where they stood to decay along the roadside. It was a sight that forever ruined the pristine beauty of the woods; not just in the winter time but summer as well. By the time summer had arrived that year I had not minded living on the farm at all. In fact, I had grown to love it.

Like all newly married couples, we had hoped by summer to start a family. Ten months into our marriage family members were asking, "Got anything started yet?" Of course, that meant a baby! Finally, in July I kept an appointment with the obstetrics department at Geisinger where I worked. I was thrilled to learn that I was pregnant. I remember stopping at Cain Pharmacy to pick up a vitamin prescription. While I waited for Mr. Cain to fill my order, I looked around at all the baby things. It was a thrill beyond words! Then I spotted the tiny baby rattles. There were blue ones and pink ones in various shapes and sizes all tied with a pink or blue bow. I chose a pink diaper pin shaped one with which to announce the news to my husband. I laid it next to his supper plate that evening when I had set the table. After I broke the news, we were both thrilled. I continued to work at my full-time job in the dietary office at the hospital where our baby would be born the following April.

However, three months into my pregnancy I began to have spotted bleeding. Immediately I phoned my obstetrician. After seeing me, he did not think the bleeding to be anything serious. The morning sickness never let up. It didn't have any preference as to morning, noon, or evening. I continued to experience irregular bleeding. I was very concerned about losing the baby.

That October I was home alone when a vast early snowstorm developed. His parents were away and Lawrence was hauling milk. I was terrified and kept watching the road for either the milk tanker or my in-law's car to come around the turn of the road. The snow continued to sweep the farm; the wind howled whirling gusts around our mobile home. I continued to watch the road late into the day. Finally, they had arrived. I felt a huge burden lifted. After all, this was my first winter on the farm and it was not at all like living in town where we had close neighbors.

Soon my obstetrician signed orders for me to leave my job. I felt a sense of relief that I no longer had to live a scheduled life. I would have been leaving my job anyway when the baby was born. During the pregnancy, I went into premature labor twice. I was very worried that I might miscarry the baby. I can't say why I thought the baby would be a girl but, from the beginning, I had a sense that it was a she. Perhaps, in part, because I had a girl's name picked out from the time I was around thirteen years old. I held the name in secret all those years.

On Sundays when my husband wasn't hauling milk, I'd bake meatloaf, macaroni and cheese, and some dessert. We'd pack everything in the car and drive around the countryside exploring back roads. In the fall we drove through forests taking in the bright sunshine and colored leaves in all their glorious hues of red, orange, gold, yellow and bronze. The pungent air wafted through our windows mingling with the aroma of meatloaf. Sometime around noon, we'd park the car along a road where mountain laurel and white birch trees dotted the banks. I'd get out the food, paper plates, and drinks.

Sometimes, on a hot day, we'd spot a picnic table somewhere nestled in the woods. On colder days we ate in the car. In winter, our drives could take us to Raymond B. Winter State Park, located within Bald Eagle State Forest or Ricketts Glen State Park. A journey to Eagles Mere might have found us stopping at the toboggan slide. Despite the cold, there were always folks enjoying the icy thrills of wintertime.

During the spring and summer months, our Sunday afternoon drives might find us traveling to the Pocono Mountains or just checking out various farms and farmlands on back roads. Invariably, we'd take hot dogs and rolls, potato salad, and other picnic goodies in our basket and seek out a roadside rest. Our grill was nothing more than a metal pot-shaped thing, but it served the purpose. The pre-children days of our lives were indeed unique and were, somehow, a nice foundation for our marriage in the ensuing years. Best of all, I had discovered that marriage is far more than love. It's a commitment, one we had made and kept.

Shake Me I Rattle

In December 1962 even at age twenty-one, I was still shy. The annual Aurand family Christmas party was always held at Grammy Aurand's house at 618 Bloom Street in Danville the last Sunday before Christmas. My husband was the eldest of Grandma and Grandpa Aurand's grandchildren; thus I was the first granddaughter-in-law to show up at the gathering pregnant. Since the doctors feared our baby wasn't growing on schedule, I had not yet donned maternity clothes. However, for this special event, I was eager to try them out. In those days they were "two-piecies," the top and the skirt with a big hole below the waist to allow room for baby, then tied in a bow at the waist with a drawstring. It was a whole new experience for me. I remember feeling a bit awkward in that outfit. We parked the car on Academy Avenue next to a tall snow-covered pine tree and walked the short distance to the house. As we entered, the aroma of Christmas dinner filled the air. We had pulled names the previous Thanksgiving and placed our gifts under the brightly lit tree. Somehow I felt warmly accepted in my maternity duds. After all everyone had by now heard that Lawrence and Kay were expecting a baby.

The meal was buffet style, each family providing a covered dish or two. Grandma Aurand had a long table in her kitchen. I guess you could call it a sideboard. Letting the children go first, we lined up ogling the layout of sliced turkey, rich brown gravy, spicy meatballs, and mashed potatoes. Mingled among the dishes were scalloped potatoes, creamed corn, macaroni and cheese, and raw veggies. There was an array of mouth-watering desserts including country-baked rice pudding and Grandma's favorite lemon fluff. After much conversing and catching up on each others' lives, the children eagerly passed out the gifts we had placed under the tree. The kids received toys and played with them on the living room carpet. We adults showed off our presents. It was an especially memorable Christmas. Grandma and Grandpa Aurand were running out of space for the growing family. Soon it would be held at someone else's home where we would begin a new chapter of the annual Aurand family Christmas parties.

I was happy and excited, in particular, since our baby was coming in April. What better time, I thought, than spring when I could take him or her for buggy walks on the country roads. And, as he grew, show him the animals on the farm. At that time some of the milk cows names were: Sparrow, Blackie, Flights, and Big Bag. The radio was always on during milking time as cows always give better to music. There were so many things to discover on the farm.

Over time I learned the names of each piece of farm machinery. We had our own eggs and our own butcherin,' as Pennsylvania farmers refer to curing their own cows or pigs. Thanks to our herd of Holsteins we had our own milk. Our weekly grocery shopping totaled between $8.00 and $8.50. My cart was filled at the supermarket checkout. The grocery bill remained at those prices for quite a long time as compared to these days when food costs appear to increase by the week.

The new year arrived, and I was relieved, twice, to have been spared premature labor with medication. My nausea never let up, but I was learning to control it with Saltines and eating more slowly. I can't tell you whether it was psychological or if one's mental thoughts weigh into the outcome of a pregnancy. But for several years, even before I had married, I had this inner suspicion that I would lose my first baby. In truth, I hesitate to even reveal this because I was guilt-ridden when it happened. I cannot tell you the source of my thoughts; I know only that it was real. The last thing I would have wanted was for my baby to die.

Today, whenever I recall my "premonition," the guilt I feel causes me to wonder the outcome had I known Jesus in a personal relationship. Perhaps had I been awakened spiritually, I would have had better tools for thwarting such thoughts. At the same time, due to past disappointments and tragedy, I struggled to believe that something good could happen to me. In my lifetime I had never revealed this anomaly to anyone; not even my husband. My only solace in escaping the guilt is knowing that my baby had gone to heaven and I will see her again one day. I share this now because I want you to know that you can be set free from demonic forces. Our Bible tells us in Ephesians 6:11—"Put on the whole armor of God, that ye may be able to stand against the wiles of the devil."

February 6, 1963 was a Monday. My husband was doing barn chores when I began to feel the pain. I wanted to disbelieve it was labor, but the pain was going through my back. I couldn't deny it. My husband came in from the barn, and we called the hospital. The nurse instructed, "Come to the emergency room now." By the time I'd reached the hospital, the labor had gone too far to halt. From the emergency room, I was transferred to one of the examining rooms while my husband was directed to a waiting room. I was, by then, in excruciating pain. It seemed like hours I groaned; then I was taken to the delivery room. Around 11:56 AM our baby was born. I asked Dr. Nicodemus what it was. He said solemnly, "Female." I thought, "Oh, a girl." Then he warned me that she probably would not make it. I heard one of the attendants say, "Get the pediatrician up here right away." As I lay in stunned silence, I could sense Dr. Suddarth working on our baby and I thought I heard a machine of some sort running. Still today I can recall that "pumping" sound. It lasted about an hour, and I thought they had given up. I was then wheeled to a room on the maternity floor. Our baby had been taken to the nursery in an isolette. Valerie Susan Derr weighed two pounds, one ounce. She lived less than an hour.

Before her death, I was given a choice to see her, or not, and whether or not I wanted her baptized by the nurse "who had the authority." Or, did I want them to call a minister? I was in a blur. My decision to not see her, I think, was due in part to the relief I felt that the past seven months of nausea were over. Today having a premature baby is drastically different from the way it was in the 1960s. Nowadays stillborn babies are held, family members cherishing each second, dreading the finality of handing the baby over to professionals.

How I wish there had been more education on the importance of psychological healing when the outcome for one's newborn is not good. I am reasonably sure I was not the first mother who lives with the deep regret of never seeing, nor comforting, her premature baby and I doubt I was the last. Now when I look at babies born at twenty-nine weeks I am reminded of how my baby must've looked when she was born. At the time, however, my knowledge was limited to that of my imagination.

I can't tell you how much I later regretted my decision. In those days, it seemed like the right thing to do. I was to guess that somehow it made it easier if my choice was to not see her. Then I was asked, "Do you want the funeral director to come for your baby or should we take care of her here?" In a daze, I said, "Well, I guess you can just take care of her here." I did not even know what that meant! All the while my husband was still in the waiting room. When he finally came into my room he simply walked to a window and looked out. I don't think he knew how to react at that moment.

My mom was working that day in the housekeeping department. She and her friend, Vivian, came in to see me. It was then Vivian said, "Kay, take your baby and bury her. One day you will have other children and you will want to have a place in which to show them her memorial." Vivian said she had also lost a baby, but later had a son. She was able to take him and show him where his sister had been buried. A sense of relief swept over me. After Mom and Vivian left the room, I called the nurse. I held my breath fearing it might be too late. Thankfully, they had not yet taken her. To this day I am deeply grateful that there was a delay and that my husband had the chance to phone Mr. Fermier. Bill had always been our family's funeral director.

My mom suggested we bury our baby on top of my dad's burial. On a cold winter day, my husband went with the funeral director to bury our baby. Mr. Fermier told him that he'd "put a little kimono on her." Sun streamed through my hospital room window from where I could see the hill; the cemetery where my baby was being laid to rest. I went home empty-handed and with a broken heart when the song, "Shake Me I Rattle Squeeze Me I Cry," was popular and every time I heard it I ached for my little Valerie.

Tearful Eyes

Damp, chilly days lingered as did the pain in my heart. Trying to find ways to get past the hurdle of winter weather after having lost my baby girl, Valerie, was a challenge. It seemed that all of my God-given talents such as painting, needlework, and crafts could not entice me and, even if they had, they left me feeling unfulfilled.

Then my mother-in-law did something I thought extraordinary. She brought a big cardboard box of old Aurand family photos, and I spent hours looking at my husband's maternal family members at all stages of their lives. Among family members of whom I was already acquainted were those who had long since passed away. In particular, I enjoyed the pictures of her and her siblings growing up on the farm in Jerseytown, Pennsylvania. I had heard her talk about those days, but seeing the photos definitely enhanced her stories. Her caring thoughtfulness proved to be the perfect remedy for passing some of the time. I have never forgotten this vignette which proved to be just the right therapy I needed at the time.

Finally, it was spring! Yellow tulips I had planted the previous year began to peek their lovely heads through the ground around our mobile home. It may seem silly but, from my living room window, I sensed a strange comfort as Whitey and Big Bag grazed in the pasture along with the other cows. I had found some white paint and painted the fence that separated our yard from the cow pasture. Spring was a breath of fresh air. No pun intended! I found much pleasure in transferring iris rhizomes from a plot on the farm to several other locations which I thought needed a bit of cheer. To this day they bloom each spring along the corn crib. Soon I had changed my favor for sweet peas to tall bearded iris. Few flowers come in so many colors, each bearing pretty names such as "Chocolate Kiss," "Blueberry Bliss," and "Stepping Out."

Also that first spring on the farm I had my initial lesson on helping call the cows for milking time. I learned that you merely shout "Come boss...come boss." Once in the barn, I helped with the milking chores. Since I had not grown up on a farm, I never learned to milk cows. My job was merely forking hay to them in their stanchions and carrying the buckets of milk to the milk tank. About the only thing I liked about milking time was the cats. They never failed to show up at milking time; thus I had to fight their pawing at my legs for their turn to lap milk from the dish. I enjoyed holding my favorite charcoal colored cat, a male I named Charlie. However, after several years, one spring Charlie had kittens! It was a rude awakening to discover Charlie was not a male.

Summer was soon to follow, and country roadside walks helped fill the hours surprising me with a sampling of wild berries on the banks; never mind a slight dappling of dust. Most every fourth evening I rode along with my husband on his milk route. In truth, though it was daylight saving time, I did not like being alone at night time. The hours stretched out, but I enjoyed seeing the countryside and the unique features each farm held.

Most memorable was the farmer who had geese. It was always a challenge for Lawrence to get back into the truck as the geese nipped at his pants.

While my husband hauled bulk milk, he had four days off each summer. In July we took a trip to Cape Cod. As we drove along the highways and byways strains of Patti Page's "Old Cape Cod" song of the l950s filled my head. I was seventeen when it was a hit and, whenever I heard the song on the radio, I longed to see the quaint little villages and the ocean view. The melody and the words were sweet but, more so, romantic. We stopped at various eating places though I don't recall an ocean view at any of those we visited. Undoubtedly, they didn't match our pocketbook.

It was in Cape Cod that we had seen our first hippie. In a restaurant, no less. In the early hippie years, there were no signs that read: "No shoes. No shirt. No Service" in the windows of most restaurants. Thus this hippie was neither shod nor shorn.

We spent some time on the beach; my husband in his red and green plaid swimming trunks and me in my lime green bathing suit. Though touring the sights was more our cup of tea. We had learned early not to drive into the sand after seeing many vehicles stuck; needing to be towed. I'm sure the tow companies reaped a harvest as a result of drivers getting stuck in the sand. There were no warning signs that I recall.

I mailed a five cent postal card to my former office workers at the Geisinger dietary department stating that McDonald's hamburgers were thirty-five cents. Hamburgers in Danville were only fifteen cents. A Coca-Cola was a dime in Pennsylvania in l963; but more at Cape Cod. Sure it was a resort, but we small town folk thought it stunning that a McDonald's hamburger could be thirty-five cents! After driving

75

around the area for a day or so, our four days were up. It was time to return to Pennsylvania and life on the farm.

In the summer of 1963, Jacqueline and John Kennedy were expecting their third child. Patrick Bouvier Kennedy was the first baby born to a sitting President and first lady since the nineteenth century. Born prematurely in August their son died just thirty-nine hours after his birth, a victim of what was then the most common cause of death among premature infants— hyaline membrane disease. I identified, having lost our little Valerie to respiratory distress syndrome.

That same year, Kyu Sakamoto, a twenty-one-year-old Japanese pop idol released a hit record, "Sukiyaki." Born on December 10, 1941, Kyu Sakamoto, at the age of 43 died in a plane crash that killed 520 people on August 12, 1985, near Tokyo, Japan. In a sense, the song echoed the sadness of my heart over the loss of our baby daughter. I walked with tearful eyes.

Over those warm months, I had prayed for another baby. I remembered that Aunt Ann and Uncle Bingy had buried an infant girl early in their marriage. As it turned out, Phyllis was the only child to come into their lives. "Please God, don't let me be like Aunt Ann and never have another child," I begged. Soon it was fall. As the leaves fell from the trees, I felt as though my heart had died with them. Christmas arrived, and I envisioned our little girl as she would have been ten months old; nearly ready to walk. I thought of the doll she might have received "from Santa." A baby that when shaken would have rattled and, when squeezed would have cried. But I could not bring Valerie home to love.

The holidays had passed and we faced another bitterly cold January. But in the bleakness of those cloudy days, there was a bright spot. My husband's birthday was January 26 and we had gone to Farmers Best restaurant in Lewisburg in celebration.

We were seated at a table next to the fireplace, the crackling fire radiating warmth dispelling the cold of the chilly night air. His birthday proved to be a time of healing. The ambiance of the fire warmed my spirit. I felt a sense of hope as we looked forward to a new year.

Soon the March winds began to blow announcing my soon-coming birthday. We, again, went to Farmers Best for my celebration. After our dinner next to the crackling coals in the fireplace, we spent some time in the gift shop.

By June I was reasonably certain I had been pregnant again. Then came the morning sickness. Thankfully this time it held to mornings only. To curb nausea, I ate a couple of Saltines before getting out of bed. Following an appointment with obstetrics, I learned our baby would be born in November. This time I had not sensed any particular gender one way or the other. It didn't seem to matter.

September arrived, and it was hot! As much as I hated the winter, I was never so glad to see November come. It is always nice to have a baby on some particular day or a family member's birthday. My father-in-law's birthday was December 1, however, so no chance of hitting his birthday. Or so I thought. Our baby was going to be born around November 21. Several days passed and December 1 was drawing closer. My father-in-law offered me $20 if I had "him" on his birthday.

December 1 was a Tuesday. It was a night of watching television. My husband and I never missed *The Red Skelton Show*. Red Skelton was a class act. Not only a gifted comedian, he rightfully boasted that it was unnecessary to use foul language and coarse jokes to make people laugh. I both respected and loved Red Skelton! My husband commented during the show, "If this doesn't bring it on, nothing will!" The show ended. We headed for bed. Just as I hit the bedroom, my water broke. Lawrence, in his haste and excitement, caught the edge of the metal bed leg and badly stubbed his toe. We grabbed my suitcase and headed for the car.

Arriving at the emergency room, I was wheeled to the elevator. In my excitement, I must've hyperventilated. I shook all the way to the labor and delivery floor. While I was in labor, I was hooked up to a machine. The nurse said it was "caudle." I had never heard of it, but it was perfectly okay with me. I felt no pain and, if I hadn't known it, would never have thought I was in labor.

I was then wheeled into the delivery room. By then it was around 11:00 PM. I remember telling my obstetrician to hurry, that it was my father-in-law's birthday. He assured me, "That's up to the baby." Greg Allen Derr arrived at 11:36 PM. I couldn't believe it! He weighed 7 pounds, 8 ounces and was in perfect health. The baby was taken to meet his dad in the waiting room, as was the custom in those days. Then it was off to the nursery for him, and to a room for me. Lawrence awakened his parents when he got back to the farm. Of course, my father-in-law owed me $20! The next day my mother-in-law picked Greg out in the nursery without looking at the baby name on his bassinet.

Like most mothers, I wanted to be the best mom as possible. Seven days later when I left the hospital, the staff included "a book of directions" by Johnson's Child Development, *Your Child from Birth to Six Months*. Six months later, I received a copy of *Your Child from Six Months to One Year.* In earnest, I had read the books, and re-read them. Little had I known then that my baby came with a real book of directions. The author— Jesus Christ—Who created him! Who else knew more about how to raise a child than his Maker? Instructions which I had yet to discover.

Christmas shopping that year in downtown Danville was a

delight. Lawrence and I bought plush animals, squeaky toys, and new baby boy clothing. It had been a long-awaited and fun Christmas. We couldn't wait to take him to the Aurand family Christmas party. Lawrence's Aunt Dorothy had a son also that year. Jamie was only about ten weeks older than Greg. When the two boys were a year old, the Christmas party was held at Aunt Joanne's and Uncle Bob's home.

In late winter 1965, Lawrence and I began searching for a house. We'd outgrown our mobile home and looked at three homes. One, we decided, was too close to the main highway. The second home wasn't exactly what we wanted. A third had been surrounded by the foundation for the new Interstate 80 short way, rendering the location highly undesirable.

As we looked at homes, we considered the option of building a house on some farm acreage which Lawrence's parents had offered. We chose a plot in the woods. However, during the process of clearing brush and trees, we encountered two snakes. They may, or may not, have been copperheads but we didn't want to take the chance. We opted for a spot on a hill which offered a beautiful view and gorgeous sunsets. After selecting a builder and settling on the plans, the ground was broken for our new home.

Each evening around sunset we checked the progress. I remember envisioning a fire in the fireplace which was taking shape and the Christmas holidays we would celebrate in our new home. Soon installation for the bow window had begun; I was very eager to make the color selections of the various rooms. I chose Autumn Tan for the bathroom fixtures and Oatmeal Spice, a speckled glaze for the tile. We began shopping for kitchen appliances at various stores. I will always remember one such fascinating demonstration. We had gone to Sears in Bloomsburg. A customer service representative showed us their selection. We were awed as he reached for a carpet sweeper and placed it under one refrigerator. When he turned the sweeper on, lo and behold, the refrigerator rose leaving enough space to clean under it!

We did not, however, go for that model since we had a cupboard above the refrigerator. Finally, we decided on General Electric. Turquoise, Harvest Gold, and Coppertone were popular color choices that year. We chose Turquoise. Our new electric range had a self-cleaning oven; a relatively new feature at that time. It also had a grill which fit over two of the burners. Over two decades I made a ton of buckwheat cakes on that beautiful grill. Our new kitchen boasted an automatic dishwasher; also fairly new in those days. A bar separated the kitchen from the family room. Greg was yet small enough to walk under the bar; a sweet memory. The following Christmas Lawrence's parents gave us two beautiful, sturdy wooden bar stools. It became the perfect place for me to reconcile the checkbook and pay bills, licking each envelope and adding a five-cent postage stamp.

We chose a fieldstone fireplace which provided many years of crackling fires. We had three nice-sized bedrooms, each with its own closet and bi-fold doors. No "en-suite" bathrooms in those days! The exterior front of our home was white brick. It was actually more an orange colored brick with a whitewash. Our house had a flagstone floor foyer with a big coat closet. I chose an elegant amber globe light fixture for the entryway. The front doors were double. We painted them black. Each early evening we went to examine the progress of our home. Greg played on the piles of dirt, running up one side and down the other in his little pastel corduroy coveralls, Buster Brown shirts, and white Pro-Tek-Tiv shoes.

On September 3, 1966 we moved into our newly built home. While I cleaned dishes and put things away, my mother-in-law helped keep an eye on Greg. It was, indeed, a most exciting time for us. We placed Greg's crib in the bedroom facing the road, while Lawrence and I claimed the master bedroom facing the backyard. The third bedroom awaited a future fourth member of our family.

Christmas was a thrilling time in our new home. I baked chocolate chip cookies, sugar cookies in various animal shapes sprinkled with colored sugar, and peanut butter cookies topped with Hershey kisses. A fresh cut Christmas tree sparkled in front of our bow window. Its multicolored blinking lights formed a shadow on the ceiling at night time. It was calming watching its repeated pattern as I relaxed on our gold velvet couch in the evening. The scent of pine filled our living room.

Santa came down our chimney that year and, of all things, he'd torn his suit! I took home movies of Greg's glee as he spotted the red cloth among the firewood. Santa had brought Little Golden books, a pull toy cow that went "moo" when its head was lifted with the string, a Fisher Price Ferris wheel, a new blue snowsuit and all manner of toys for toddlers.

Christmas that year was scarred only by my sorrow knowing our soldiers were fighting an awful war in the jungles of Vietnam. Here I was in my new home, I thought, and there they were fighting a hideous war so that we might experience freedom. A freedom that meant they were sacrificing Christmas with their loved ones. My heart died each time I saw the day's war news on television. There were demonstrations of various booby traps concocted by the Viet Cong, including one which burned intensely into my conscience. It was a wall of nails intended for our soldiers which, when tripped, flung their bodies into the long spikes. It was horrific.

During the summer of 1967, we added a cement patio in front of the sliding glass doors of our family room. Black wrought iron railings surrounded the deck. While poring over seed catalogs, I educated myself in all manner of flowers and dreamed of landscaping the exterior of our new house. In due time I ordered arborvitae bushes for the front of our home. I chose perennials, including citrus-scented green bells of Ireland. However my favorite flowers were iris, and I ordered many tall bearded varieties, including a very special iris, "Eliza Kay." Somehow I likened the name to mine and my birth mother's name, Elizabeth. Amid the iris, I had placed flat rocks which we had saved from the excavation of our home. Among all the gay varieties of gorgeous flowers, I selected roses for around the new patio.

That summer I ordered Seafoam floribunda rose bushes from Spring Hill Nursery in Ohio from where I had mail ordered the perennials and daylily bulbs. The Seafoam roses were a lovely light salmon color. They took off speedily, and soon sweet rose perfume permeated the air around the deck.

Cherished are the photos I took of Greg, wearing his red plaid sunsuit, riding his new tricycle I had gotten with S & H green stamps. Red, white and blue streamers flowed from the handlebars of his shiny red trike. I can still see him flying around in circles, his blonde hair whipping in the breeze. He loved riding it on the flat surface of the new patio.

Grass finally grew. Lawrence bought Greg his own little plastic lawn mower so he could "help his dad mow." We watched as Greg started "mowing" across the grass along the front sidewalk. All of a sudden he flung the mower into the air. "It doesn't cut!" he demanded. We couldn't help but laugh realizing that he'd thought his new mower was going to do the job!

Our home, having been located on the farm, was surrounded by wooded areas providing a show of beautiful fall foliage. Soon the leaves turned from chartreuse, clover, and sap green to shades of autumn gold, Indian red, pumpkin orange, peach, and salmon. How glorious!

While we had planted a postage-stamp plot of dwarf fruit trees, we had yet to plant ornamentals. Our fruit trees, in the ensuing years, provided us with an abundance of sour and sweet oxheart cherries. The following year I placed orders for a golden chain tree, a pink dogwood, a honey locust, and my favorite—a mimosa tree. I chose to plant the mimosa tree between our patio and the exterior of our white brick fireplace. I had yet to learn that Gary would be born in 1968 and would one day, with the neighbor boys, sleep starry nights under the canopy of the mimosa tree. Its long green fronds provided a tropical-like setting. Its flamingo pink feathery flowers exploded like showering fireworks. The scent was intoxicating!

October, 1967 I became pregnant with our second son. Gary Lee Derr was born August 4, 1968 weighing 8 pounds, 4 ounces. I had been so confident that the new baby was going to be a boy that my mother-in-law quipped, "I think you'd have been disappointed if he hadn't been a boy!" We received many new baby boy greeting cards. Among them was one I'll always remember. Olive Clark had been my Sunday school teacher at the church adjacent to our farm. Olive wrote on her card, "What could be nicer than one boy? Why two boys!" Her card remains among my treasury of memories. Letting go of things from our boys' childhood days was not easy. I was to learn letting go would come much sooner than I had expected.

My sentiments are best expressed in one of my favorite Christmas songs, *Heirlooms* by Amy Grant. Stored in our attic were their high chair, wooden playpen, and the combination buggy/stroller I received from Mom at Greg's baby shower. Among the rafters lay some of their favorite toys—the cow that went "moo" when its head was lifted. There was also a variety of Fisher-Price toys which I had not seen in a long time. There was an airplane, a merry-go-round, a garage and more, each with its own set of little wooden people. So much had I cherished their preschool years that I saved many of their baby clothing items on little blue plastic hangers and reattached the tags. Later when my first grandson, Gary, was born I gave all those nearly-new baby clothes to his parents.

After our son Gary was born I taught myself to crochet. I crocheted many baby items including a mint green sunsuit. I had him photographed wearing the fruits of my labor. I crocheted a huge stuffed yellow duck big enough for the boys to sit on. Growing up on a farm meant that boys had snowmobiles. They also helped with barn chores. They never complained about wearing the knitted ski masks I made them. I recall one of them was a colorful mask with Indian "feathers" sticking from the top of the cap. As the boys grew, I sewed them many matching outfits including suits with red and white stars on a Navy fabric. They wore them on a Fourth of July vacation.

When Gary was around twelve years old, I crocheted a gold poncho with a big horseshoe fastener. Never mind that girls mainly wore ponchos, he was sold on the big cowboy buckle and happily wore his poncho. Greg was around the same age when he asked me to continue sewing corduroy pants. Though they were boy pants, I made them with an elastic waist which he preferred over store purchased pants. When he went to college he needed a laundry bag. You might have guessed. Mom made him a big black corduroy bag with double stitching and a drawstring closure.

On Cameltown Hill Road we had neighbors we knew from our high school days. Over the years, we spent some good times with the three families. Parties, picnics, attending the Bloomsburg Fair and more. Their children and our boys were friends over those many years on the farm. In those days our dogs ran freely on the hill, and no one complained. I always referred to them as "his, mine, and ours." Among them was our dog, Smokey, and the Stigerwalt boys' dog, Max.

A dirt road lined one of the farm fields near our house. The lane led into the woods where the Weaver family, Hilda and her sons, Bobby and "Shorty," had taken up residence. Over several decades my husband plowed the road for them in winter snows. We helped them as much as possible. One Thanksgiving Day an unrelenting snowstorm hit Danville and its surroundings. Very few homes, if any, had electricity that day. No one could cook Thanksgiving dinner. The following day I went to see how Hilda was making out after the storm. Inviting me into her kitchen, she said, "We don't have much, but we had Thanksgiving dinner!" Hers was a wood burning stove!

When Gary was around ten years old, he suggested, "Dad, I want to make a birdhouse." His dad helped him craft a shelter box for a little feathered friend. When it came time to paint it, he wondered what color he should use. As it turned out, all we could find was a small can of lavender paint. When the paint had dried, we decided to hang it on the golden chain tree in front of our home. The tree flowered profusely in the summer with its beautiful cascading yellow blossoms. I was careful not to mention it to Gary, but never in my wildest dreams did I think a bird would choose a lavender birdhouse! It was, furthermore, sitting crooked on the branch.

To my amazement, I looked one day to discover a pair of bluebirds had taken up residence in Gary's birdhouse! That spring I watched the birds fly from electrical overhead wires to their little lavender abode as they fed their fledglings. Even more surprising was that they returned year after year. That is, until the year my husband was no longer there. Nor was I. In a few short years I will have sold my cherished home on the farm.

Today I have a lifetime of memories cut far too short by my

husband's illness and death on April 29, 1984. We never celebrated a silver wedding anniversary.

**My adoptive Dad holding me
on the skunk farm
1943**

**My adoptive parents
Mom, Dad, Linda, Kay
1948**

View from the skunk farm

Mom in our kitchen - 1958

**Dad, the bungalow he built,
railroad shed, and Forney coal yard in rear**

Me - age 12

**My mother, little Kenny, the house
behind Shooters Bar**

**My father, a patient at a
sanatorium**

My brother, Kenneth Lee Beyer

Little Kenny with our mother

My mother, Elizabeth, and her mother, Bertha Wray Stetler

My grandparents, Moses and Bertha Wray Stetler

**My father's artwork, pen and ink drawings, and two of the
Danville High School yearbook cartoons**

90

Lawrence Allen Derr

Sylvia Kay Stetler Derr

My mother, Grace, and me

Clowning on Easter - 1983

Thomas "Grampy" Wray

Mr. Ed and Mrs. Helen Stahl

91

Lawrence in 1961

Me in Kalamazoo in 1991

**Lawrence in our kitchen
early 80s**

Our boys in the 70s

**Our five grandchildren
Matt, Charissa, Maddie, Gary, John**

Lawrence - late 50s

My son, Greg, and Kelly

My husband and Greg 1965

**Greg on his S&H
green stamp trike**

Greg - 1966

House Greg built

**Greg with Pap
Their December 1 birthday**

My son, Gary, and Arlene met in the nursery
Arlene born August 3, Gary born August 4, 1968
Right: Arlene, Gary and me-2011

Gary and Arlene - 1986

House Gary built

Gary Lee Derr

Gary farms the homestead farm

94

Jeremy and Charissa White - married 7-29-2017

Briar Lee White born July 18, 2018

Greg holding Charissa

**Greg's Gram Derr - my
mother-in-law holding Charissa**

Madelyn Quinn life-guarding

Maddie's gymnast competition in Baltimore

Ryleigh - pool time

Maddie and Ryleigh

Greg-Maddie-Ryleigh June 11, 2017

Ryleigh Quinn First snow 11-17-18

Gary and Chelsie 10-22-2011

Chelsie and Gary

Gary, Chelsie and children

Troy and Del, in middle, at their adoption

Troy Del Dominik

Delavan Dominik Troy

John and Mandi - Marine Ball   **John and Mandi 9-15-2018**

Mandi and John   **Checking the roof of his real estate listing**

John William - 1994   **Mandi's graduation from Kutztown University**

Matthew Allen Derr

Matt - 1994

Brittany and Matt

**Matt farms and works for
Valley Township with his dad**

Matt on the roller

Snowmobiling on the Derr farm

Levi and Melissa Beyer home   **Levi and Melissa Flick Beyer**

Levi VanHorn Beyer's Meat Wagon

Big Mill in Danville, Pennsylvania circa 1895

Ace Cleaner school

R - Grandmother Carrie Beyer
L - Olive Beyer, her daughter

My father, Kenneth Lee Beyer, and Dick Elliot who died in WWII

My brother, Kenneth Lee Beyer

My grandmother
Carrie Lawn Earp Beyer

101

Mom, Grace, 1957

Lawrence and Kay

My house in Kalamazoo

My ice skates

**L - Dad Joseph (Chub)
R - Uncle Raymond (Raym)
My mother, Elizabeth, in rear**

**Dad, Chub - Mom, Grace
on the skunk farm
1941**

While the rose blows along the river brink,
With old Khayyám the Ruby Vintage drink:
And when the Angel with his darker draught
Draws up to thee—take that, and do not shrink.

My father drew this as a high school project when he was 18 years old.

Verse from Omar Khayyam's *The Rubaiyat*

God has said: "Today I am giving you a choice between good and evil, between life and death." Deuteronomy 30:15

The question is: Will you choose the cup offered by Jesus Christ—eternity in God's heaven OR will you drink of the deadly curse offered by Satan—eternity in Satan's hell?

Life is like a Tapestry

It wasn't a "normal" rain. Multiple times, through the night, I had been awakened by the thunderous sound of rain. The previous spring brought many showers; the ground was already drenched. June 21, 1972, we'd gone to bed to pouring rain. Each time I was awakened, I remarked to my husband, "Listen to that rain."

In 1972 Hurricane Agnes roared through every town along the Susquehanna River. Around 2 AM I got up to help Lawrence get around for work. His job that day hauling bulk milk was to have taken him to the area of Montoursville, about thirty-three miles north of our home. Lawrence went out the door through our basement which was our habit when headed out. In a jiffy, he came back up the steps to alert me, "You'd better try to get your things up. There's water in the cellar." How could we have that much water in our basement, I wondered. Our home was on a hill and, in truth, I don't recall ever having water in the basement. If so, it had been merely surface water.

At the time I had a small craft business. There were various tables and wooden spools throughout the room used to display my handicrafts. I rushed to move everything possible to a higher level. By daybreak, while listening to the local radio station, I realized there were damaging floods all over the area. The boys helped me sweep water from the cellar into the driveway. We made multiple sweeps that day and, despite my arms being tired, we were forced to keep shoving the water out of the basement.

By afternoon, Lawrence made a collect phone call to let me know how serious the flooding had become and that he may not make it home that night. It seems Lycoming Creek was over its banks and that is where he was at the time. In the ensuing hours, the flooding became what was then known as the costliest hurricane to hit the United States in recorded history. Hurricane Agnes howled through the valley destroying everything in its path. The most significant effects, by far, occurred in Pennsylvania due to flooding.

While the Scranton/Wilkes Barre area suffered the majority of the damage, the flood's fury created a scenario that would take months, even years, from which to recover. In the days that followed Hurricane Agnes, we came to realize just how significantly our town was inundated. No one was permitted to enter many areas of town until the water began to recede. After rescue workers had completed the initial stages of getting everyone to safety we were allowed to travel the main route into downtown Danville. It was stunning to see that a landmark stone arched bridge over Mahoning Creek was lost.

All or most of Danville's second ward was underwater. Though the Susquehanna River has flooded our town multiple times over its history, it seemed incredible that rescuers were using motor boats on our downtown Mill Street. Many of Danville's shops had water up to one's waist. The new Danville High School, from which my class was the first to graduate in 1959, was inundated. I remember having a hard time accepting that those lovely red velvet cushioned seats in the auditorium were now in ruins. All, or nearly all, mobile homes in the second ward were destroyed. Aunt Mary, Uncle Dave and their daughter, Debbie, along with their dog "Lucky," were rescued by boat. Lawrence and I brought them to our house. Little had we realized then that it would be six months until they were able to find suitable housing. Somehow it seemed that having my aunt, uncle, and Debbie in our home made up for those days in 1959 after Dad committed suicide. They had taken us in until we were emotionally well enough to return to our home in Riverside.

Once authorities permitted entrance into town, I drove my aunt and uncle to their mobile home. They were shocked to see all the damage. Nearly everything they owned was gone, but we managed to salvage some clothing. While it was of no real importance, just a few days before the flood I had loaned Debbie my Cosmetology Handbook. What was of value were the multiple notes containing beauty secrets I learned from my instructor during evening classes. Hints that were, otherwise, not included in daytime classes. Jim was a master instructor and, while I valued my handbook with all its notes, I could not weep over such an insignificant thing when hundreds had lost everything they owned.

Many such floods have since occurred throughout the United States, but I suspect those who experienced Hurricane Agnes blazed the trail. The after-effects of such destruction can only be truly known to those who have been there. Even though our well on the farm produced little more than a gallon of water per minute, Aunt Mary and I sorted through the muddy clothing and tossed load after load into our washing machine. I had no automatic dryer back then, so my aunt and I carried the clothes to our clothesline. However, the clothes were never the same again. Truthfully, they weren't wearable. They were dark and dingy but were worn until such a time as they could be replaced. In reality, it was all a waste of time and surely had to have taxed the washing machine. Later I drove my aunt around to the multiple locations where clothing was being donated to flood victims.

That summer our two sour cherry trees had produced a bumper crop. In the throes of the flood, I didn't bother to pick them. Mary came from the old school where no one left fruits or vegetables go to waste. I remember her asking me twice, "Aren't you going to pick them?" She seemed a bit taken aback that I hadn't planned to do so. I recall Aunt Mary picking as many as she could. What she did with them I can't remember, but it appeared to be therapeutic for her after the traumatic losses.

To describe the aftermath of Hurricane Agnes and the loss of homes and businesses seems too vast to cover in a few words. I remember a favorite eating spot in Lewisburg called The Fence, a 1950s car hop, was ruined. However, it was restored and remains a very popular restaurant with a scenic river view. About a mile from The Fence a house sat in the middle of the highway, one of the thousands of homes removed from foundations. The one redeeming factor during those dark days in Pennsylvania was that the flood brought people together. Everyone pitched in to help with the cleanup.

One of the largest fairs in Pennsylvania, the Bloomsburg Fair in our neighboring town had been inundated. A high water mark was painted on one of the buildings as a reminder of Hurricane Agnes. Knoebels Amusement Resort in Elysburg, an alcohol-free park, is known as the most famous amusement park in Pennsylvania. A favorite place for multitudes of visitors each summer, Knoebels was under water as the creeks rose six feet over the banks. The flood destroyed six cottages, damaged many other buildings, twenty-four of the twenty-five rides, and the park's roller rink. It was hard to imagine how the Grand Carousel building with all the magnificent horses must have looked after the flood. The beautifully painted prancers embedded with multicolored sparkling gems, the brass ring apparatus, and calliope music now lay in a graveyard of murky flood water.

So significant were the effects of Hurricane Agnes, that the name Agnes was retired from the hurricane list in the spring of 1973. Pennsylvania, by far, experienced the most devastating damage from the flood which left a total of fifty people dead. To date, Hurricane Agnes ranks as Pennsylvania's worst disaster. While we experienced Hurricane Hazel in October 1954, which killed some 400 people in Haiti before striking the United States, I don't recall any significant damage. However, Mahoning Creek must've flooded as my Uncle Raym, apparently unable to get to his home on Bald Top after work, came to our house. He slept on the pool table in our basement. I crept down the cellar the next morning to see if he was still alive!

When Danville was back on its feet some months later, the town borough began a remapping of the 100-year floodplain. Plans for flood prevention had gone into effect. They added new levee systems, tide gates, a pumping station, and a dike along the river. Most recently flood protection was completed for the area of the former Danville High School, which is presently the Danville Middle School. A new high school and the Ironmen football field sit high on a hill near the Fairview Cemetery on the eastern part of town.

In 1975 our youngest son, Gary, was in second grade. I was looking for something more to do…some work. With somewhat of an entrepreneurial spirit, I've always been a self-starter. At the same time, I had been encouraged to relocate my basement craft business into the downtown. A little storefront opened on East Mahoning Street next door to The Danville News. The plan was that I would set closing time at 4 PM. That way I would be home by the time our boys got off the school bus at 4:15. My husband agreed to the plans. We rented the storefront from George Pappas, local owner of Pappas Restaurant. We had a sign painted—Kay's Krafts. I was ahead of myself with the craft business as craft fairs were just starting up in central Pennsylvania. The largest I had attended was located in Happy Valley, home of Pennsylvania State University. Having participated in most street fairs for some years, I sold my first oil painting at State College. It was a winter scene with a church in the background.

Soon my husband and I were offered the sale of a thriving Mill Street ceramic and craft business. Margie and John Shade gave us a fair deal on their merchandise which included the kilns and over a hundred ceramic molds. Also included was a motorized slip machine which stirred the liquid mud.

We moved the slip machine into the basement of our home, as well as the molds. I was surprised at how involved my husband was at pouring slip into the molds. There were all kinds including large and small Christmas trees. When the slip had "set" Lawrence removed the "greenware." Next, the trees were cleaned and fired. I painted the fired pieces with glaze; then loaded the kiln for a second firing. When cooled the trees were fashioned with tiny colored plastic bulbs. Finally, a tubular light was added to the base and, voila! the trees lit up in a rainbow of shades: red, green, yellow, blue, purple, and more. Each time I fired Christmas trees I could hardly wait to open the kiln to see how each had turned out.

Among a multitude of ornaments, figurines, and other bric-abrac, we also sold craft supplies and Wilton cake decorating supplies. In the 1970s jewelry-making was hugely popular. On our shop walls was all manner of beads and pearls sold by the string. Our boys were very helpful in putting shelving together, stocking shelves and helping their dad with the ceramic molding. We worked many days and nights during the years we were in business.

In the summer of 1976, I had a part-time employee who was willing to work two weeks full time while we had taken some time off. During that time my husband and I agreed to have a boy come from New York City into our home. The Fresh Air program enabled city kids to visit rural Pennsylvania for two weeks. We picked Daryl up at Bloomsburg Town Park. Daryl had come from Brooklyn along with his sister who had gone to another home which had girls in the family.

The first time we took Daryl to the barn the cows were in the pasture. Daryl pointed and asked, "What are they?" I said, "Cows. Have you never seen a cow before?" "No," he answered. It was stunning to know that a nine-year-old boy did not know what a cow looked like. Aside from the farm, we entertained Daryl by taking him on picnics, to Knoebels Amusement Resort, often for pizza, and to our church picnic at Sunnybrook Park. When Daryl did not go along to the barn with my husband and the boys, I took him for walks to the adjacent church where we had attended at the time, the Hendrickson Methodist Church, which had an adjoining cemetery.

One day as Daryl and I were sitting on the grass among the tombstones, I thought it a suitable place and time to discuss how one can know for certain that he will go to heaven. I shared with him how he could become a child of God and have the assurance that, when he dies, he will be with the Lord.

I explained that everyone has a sinful black heart, but Jesus died on the cross so that our hearts could be made white. I prayed with Daryl to invite Jesus into his heart that day at the cemetery. It was a day I well recall and, hopefully, one he has never forgotten.

It came the time, too soon, to pack Daryl's little suitcase and take him back to Bloomsburg Town Park to be joined with his sister for the bus trip back to Brooklyn. The following summer, 1977, we had registered with the Fresh Air fund to have Daryl back for a second two-week vacation. Again Tina, my part-time employee, was willing to work for two weeks at the store. It appeared Daryl was having a good time, but I think he grew homesick at times when darkness fell.

In February of 2001, I went on the Internet for the first time. It was a dream I'd had for several years and, finally, I bought my first computer. Except for some start-up lessons from the representative at Sears where I purchased my Compaq, I was self-trained. It was about that time I realized I might be able to locate Daryl through the Internet. Though I have tried at various times over the years, I have never been successful. Perhaps by some miracle, I will see him again one day. It would be wonderful to hear how he is doing. I'm sure he has not forgotten his summers on the farm as a "Fresh Air" boy.

The day came when I took my boys and left the Hendrickson Methodist Church adjacent to the Derr farm. We had attended there nearly six years. I loved teaching the kindergarten class and vacation Bible school over those years and have many happy memories attending the church.

One day a mysterious letter showed up in our mailbox. It had been mass-mailed by a self-appointed authoritarian in the church. Its content inadvertently drove more people away from the church than encouraged them to attend. To this day, I cannot

111

draw any conclusion as to its value. It did, however, serve a purpose in my life. I saw it as a direction from the Lord to seek a new church home. My husband still worked three Sundays a month so making such a choice was alright with him.

In making the move I had to consider the boys. A newspaper search for scheduled services and Sunday school times led me, with my husband's approval, to attend the St. John's United Church of Christ in Mausdale, Pennsylvania. The church was a typical red brick exterior building with a matching parsonage. The interior had a choir loft accented with white wooden pillars. Sunlight shone through the beautiful leaded stained glass windows in rays of rainbow hues. Each was inscribed as having been donated in memory of some loved one or given by members who attended in the days of the church's construction. Restrooms and the children's Sunday schoolrooms were in the basement. The adult Sunday schoolroom was next to the sanctuary. Hilda Kashner taught my class. Little had I known that Hilda would become a pertinent person in my life.

Someone who rarely attended church or Sunday school had named our class "The Jet Set." Not a very likely name, I thought, for a church class but I guess the contributor had in mind that America was in its "jet set" age of sending rockets into outer space. Each spring our class held a spaghetti supper in the basement. I enjoyed assisting in the serving.

In the sanctuary, next to the seat where I sat each Sunday, was a stained glass window. It had always caught my eye. The inscription read: "Levi and Melissa Beyer." Never in my wildest dreams could I have imagined they were my great-grandparents. At that time I had not even known I was a Beyer. As I sat in the pew, I wondered about the family who gave the beautiful gleaming window. I'm sure, at the time, Levi and Melissa would never have imagined that one day their great-granddaughter would become a member of their church and, in fact, sit next to their window on Sunday mornings. As I write this, I am still in awe when I think of that window and its connection to my life as I raised my sons attending that church.

Earlier, in 1963, construction of Interstate 80 in Valley Township, not far from the Derr family farm, had gotten underway. Until then, the dirt road traveled from the family farm directly to Route 54, the main road into downtown Danville. The road had passed by a lovely Victorian home. At times, when my husband and I traveled past the home, I commented, "I love that house."

In a million years I could not have guessed that the home and barn were part of the farm formerly belonging to my great-grandparents, Levi and Melissa Flick Beyer. Yes, the same Levi and Melissa Beyer whose family had donated the stained glass window at St. John's United Church where my family and I attended from 1972 through 1977.

Aside from farming, Levi was a businessman having sold meat from his horse-drawn wagon. Melissa was a rug weaver. Years ago the house and barn were razed making room for the Day's Inn. All that remains today are the stumps of the pine trees that dotted the farmhouse frontage. The stained glass window remains in the church at Mausdale, Pennsylvania.

While Interstate 80 was a boon for travel many homes were sacrificed for the cause. I remember the Valley Township Fire Department burned one such house along the stretch not far from our place. The DeGreen family had already vacated the home. The fire drill drew neighboring folks, including our family, to the house razing.

For many years the median of Interstate 80 had been seeded with the crown vetch plant. Crown vetch not only had beautiful foliage, but it blossomed all summer long in blankets of purple brilliance. It had spread and became, perhaps, the most beautiful highway in Pennsylvania. Regrettably, for whatever reason, it was allowed to die out. I have speculated that it had been considered a nuisance or perhaps too costly for Penn Dot to maintain. Interstate 80 is no longer robed in its former royal radiance. However, Pennsylvania's woods and state flower, the mountain laurel, beautify the many miles stretching from Ohio to New York. Eye-catching is the area of Snow Shoe in western Pennsylvania, as are the rocky mountains heading east to the Pocono Mountains. Much rock had been blasted making way for the new Keystone Shortway.

Three years ago I delved into my family tree. It was a long-anticipated hobby checked off my bucket list. As I researched, I discovered a multitude of previously unknown facts about my family; many members having immigrated to America by boat. Having settled in Bucks and Berks counties, some of them at one time or another migrated to Danville. As I travel along the various roads in my hometown, particularly those in Valley Township where Levi and Melissa made their home, I envision them in horse and buggy riding the dusty roads to church. They attended the Danville farm market and, undoubtedly, crossed the old wooden bridge which once spanned the Susquehanna River—a bridge, which was destroyed by a flood in 1905.

I've been told that my birth father rode the Montour Trolley from Danville to Riverside to visit DeWitt's Park, an amusement park in the days before the 1950s. I wonder if my father ever walked up Avenue E from the trolley stop to the park, having passed by where I would later live in the double mirror image house. I wonder, too, how many of my relatives journeyed by ferry boat on the canal, traveling as merchants from Danville to Philadelphia to sell their wares. Though my thoughts and visions remain a mystery, I feel reasonably certain they are not far-fetched.

In 1970, I kept a routine check-up appointment at our local hospital. Dr. Zimmer noticed a lump on my thyroid. I opted to have the recommended surgery right away. When I returned to the hospital for a follow-up, my doctor gave me the report. The tumor was malignant. Driving home that day was a blur. I stopped at the traffic light in front of the Montgomery House. It was then I decided that I wanted to "get myself ready for heaven." I had no idea how I was going to do that, but I continued to attend the Methodist church adjoining the family farm. My sons were two and five years old. It was important to me that they might also seek to know God.

My husband was still working three Sundays a month hauling bulk milk for the family business. I had taken our boys to Sunday school and church. I taught a class of kindergartners and read them a Bible story with visuals of Bible characters on flannelgraph every Sunday. Still, I had not discovered the Jesus for which a spark had been lit in my spirit earlier in my life.

Later we were attending the United Church of Christ in Mausdale. I, in my adult Sunday school class, and our sons each in his own Sunday school class. One day during the lesson Hilda Kashner my teacher, gesturing with her hand, instructed that Jesus could live in one's heart. It clicked! I knew at that moment that this was the key for which I had searched all my life to that point. It was that day I invited Jesus to live in my heart. The spark that had been lit early in my life burst into a flame of fire. Now Jesus was no longer someone "way over there" and I was just this someone "way over here." He was now living in my heart.

When I was about eight years old, I asked, "Mom, how do you get to heaven?" Mom said, "Well if you're good you will go to heaven." However, I was not satisfied with that instruction. While I wasn't really bad, I knew I wasn't always good. The

Bible tells us, "For all have sinned and fall short of God's expectations." Romans 3:23

Until that day in Hilda's Sunday school class I had never heard that Jesus could live in my heart. My sons also invited Jesus into their hearts as I led them in prayer at the "tuckin' in time." Now their bedtime prayers changed from "Now I lay me down to sleep" to more personal prayers. At last, I had found the way and made a decision for which every human being ever born must face. Jesus said, "I am the way, the truth, and the life. No one comes to the Father except through me."

Follow up after the surgery proved that the tumor was encapsulated and had not spread. Thus, the removal ended the malignancy. I believe that God had allowed this traumatic time in my life to bring me into a personal relationship with Jesus Christ. It is said that our lives are like a tapestry. If you look at the embroidered piece from the back side, you will find nothing but tangles and knots. But when you turn it over you unveil a beautiful tapestry.

Our town came together that summer in 1972 when a storm darkened our world along the Susquehanna River. But it changed our town in the end for the better. People supported one another. Sometimes God sends the winds and rain that we might look up and see Him through the clouds of doubt and darkness. Despite those times of tragedies in our lives, He can turn our fiery trials from ashes into rainbows of hope. We can experience victory that we might help others when they go through similar circumstances.

Perhaps you, like me, experienced missing pieces in your life due to the loss of loved ones. Or, not knowing just who you are. God can fill your life with His love and grace and help put the puzzle back together again.

Maybe you, as I had, face a diagnosis of a potentially life-threatening disease. In my case, I was keenly aware that a tumor on my thyroid might evolve into an event that might place my sons, then less than five years old, without a mother. The thought killed my spirit. However, on the day of my diagnosis, I looked up to Jesus and daily my trust in Him grew. He chose to heal me through the surgery; a second chance to seek and to serve Him throughout my lifetime. May you experience the assurance promised in Jeremiah 17: 7, 8— "Blessed is the one who trusts in the Lord, whose confidence is in Him. He will be like a tree planted by the water that sends out its roots by the stream. It does not fear when heat comes; its leaves are always green. It has no worries in a year of drought and never fails to bear fruit."

Who Am I?

Perhaps you have spent a lifetime wondering, as I had, just who you are. I never thought much about it when I was a kid. But as I matured, curiosity and questions about my ancestry not only increased but even more so when I had learned I'd been adopted. My mind was filled with questions about my past. Who was my mother, my father? What about grandparents and my other ancestors? Were they still living? If so, did they live nearby? I wanted to know everything about them—their education, accomplishments, hobbies, and more.

I was also curious about from which country I had originated. These questions bugged me much of my life. I had known my natural uncle adopted me. But in truth, I didn't know much about him other than the fact that he'd been a Danville native, was gifted in carpentry and had an outgoing personality. At the same time, I had hoped to learn who my natural father was and what he was like. I wondered, too, about my birth mother. Did she finish high school? Did she, like my sister and me, enjoy doing needlework? Would she be proud of what I've become?

Creating a family tree had been on my "bucket list," a project for when I retired. Thus, many years had passed before I finally could wait no longer to discover my roots. I chose, specifically, to write about my journey with the hopes that you might be inspired to dig into your family tree if you haven't already.

One summer day I finally began my ancestry search. Since there were so many missing pieces in my life, I didn't know where to begin. It had seemed appropriate to start with an Internet website. Though many such websites are free, only one contained what seemed to me as a file cabinet of information. Not only was there much information on my family tree, but many of those branches had already been created by other family members. I was able to glean information, documents, even photos from those trees; a legitimate and fun thing to do when researching one's family tree. It wasn't until I delved into the project that I realized just how much information is available on the Internet.

I began with a one-month subscription, which later evolved into a two-month adventure. I soon learned that a newspaper website had a considerable amount of information about my ancestors who lived in Danville and the surrounding area. I merely keyed their names into the search bar and voila! I learned dozens of details I would not have otherwise discovered about deceased family members. Among those findings was that my grandparents, Bertha and Moses Stetler, had a daughter named Frances Marion who died at age one. It had been fascinating to read about family gatherings, backyard weddings, rug weaving parties, even tidbits such as "Miss Jane Smith traveled by bus to Scranton…." and so on.

Creating a family tree is not only a fun project but addictive. I discovered that my great-grandfather, Levi Beyer, belonged to the Danville Auto Club and was contemporary with Abigail Geisinger, who was noted for owning a "Hupmobile."

Numerous newspaper articles featured the club and various auto parades in which they had participated. However, Abigail Geisinger is further famed in northeastern Pennsylvania for having founded Geisinger Medical Center in Danville. It is noted in the Geisinger Medical Center library that Abigail, a devout Christian, had set forth two directives: One, that the hospital should always remain with the Geisinger name and, two, that the Bible should never be removed from the premises.

It was fascinating to discover that my ancestors settled in Berks County and that several towns were named in their honor. Gravesites remain and, though weathered with age, most epitaphs were inscribed in the German language.

I uncovered a copy of a handwritten will by an ancestor, Jacob A. Beyer. I printed it out along with a wedding document which was signed by my great-grandparents in England. Ann Tandy had signed her name with an "X," indicating that she was probably unable to write. My husband's family tree has, to date, ended with his great-grandparents mainly because no other family members have contributed to the Derr family tree. Unless another Derr family member researches his or her ancestry, the information appears to be forever unknown.

I was delighted to discover that my husband's maternal ancestors arrived in Philadelphia on the same ship as my Beyer ancestors. Johann Phillip Beyer came to America on the *Pennsylvania Merchant*, on September 11, 1731. Added to my files is the passenger list of that voyage.

Over my lifetime I had wondered if, or how many of, my male ancestors had served in the United States military. That mystery has been primarily solved as I discovered those ancestors who served in the various wars: the Revolutionary War, the Civil War, World War I, and World War II. My maternal relative Adam M. Wray was, in fact, honored in Danville's historical archives as well as *The Bicentennial History Book.* In 1845 Adam's Columbia Guard unit was mustered in to "C," Second Pennsylvania Infantry and played a prominent role in the Mexican War:

> *The last fight of the war is on, and among the leaders of that charge are the Columbia Guards; the color bearer of the guards falls wounded, a victim of enemy fire, the battle flag falls to the earth; Adam Wray drops his gun, bends over, picks up the colors from the helpless hands of his comrade, dashes for the front of the company and the charge, spurring his comrades on by his heroic act and example, and with a faith and courage that defies the enemy fire scales the fortress, the first to plant the American colors upon the Heights of Chapultepec in a moment of victory that foretold the end of the Mexican War.*
> The Wray Family--Page 302--Danville--The Bicentennial History--Edited by Robert Phillip Bomboy

My paternal great-grandfather Earp having immigrated to America from England, suffered a leg wound in the Battle of Antietam in the Civil War. Documents have proven that he spent time in the Soldiers and Sailors Hospital in Wellsboro, Pennsylvania, as well as other hospitals serving wounded veterans.

Patriotic holidays have now become more meaningful to me as a result of discovering the history of my ancestors. I stand a bit taller when The National Anthem is rendered. Having learned from elementary school the rules for honoring the flag, I place my hand over my heart at the first note of *The Star Spangled Banner.*

The search I began in June 2015 is a lasting treasury I've left for my children, grandchildren, and future descendants. Additionally, our family tree will help future researchers whose family members intertwine with ours. Though it was very time-consuming, the effort has been gratifying. You, too, will be in for many surprises should you research your family tree. Perhaps you, like me, will have discovered who you are.

In 1970 my sister and I decided to search for our living paternal relatives. To my sister and me, finding them seemed next to impossible. We did not know where to begin.

My sister remembered Mrs. Stahl had told her the Yocums in Northumberland were our relatives. We looked up their address in the phone book and drove to Northumberland. We felt a mixture of excitement; fear of the unknown and of course how we would be received.

No one was home. We drove around for a while and decided to stop again. As we reached their driveway, a gentleman in a pick-up truck pulled in just ahead of us. He asked, "What is it I can help you with?" Silence. Then my sister blurted, "We're Lee's girls." He raised his head and cried in delight, "Ohhh." We were relieved. Then Mack excitedly led us into the house to meet his wife, Lehna. He said, "I always knew you'd come back." Remembering that affirmation still brings joy to my heart. We chatted in their living room for a time. Then Mack said, "I've got to phone Kit." When Kathryn answered he exclaimed, "You'll never guess who's here!" Kit could not wait to meet us. Malcolm (Mack), Kathryn, and Ray were our father, Lee's, first cousins.

Then Mack and Lehna made their way to stairs that led to their attic. To our surprise, they carried an armload of memorabilia that had belonged to our natural parents—Lee and Elizabeth. My sister and I shared the treasures. I kept a cedar jewelry box my father had made; having painted an oval tropical scene on the inside lid and inscribed "Elizabeth." Among other things was my father's Old Scofield Bible. After marveling over the gifts, we chatted for some time. We told them about our adoptive parents and our lives growing up in Riverside. Then Malcolm said, "Do you remember waving to the man in the caboose that went past your house?" Of course, we remembered. Then he said, "I was that man." We were flabbergasted!

Then he said, "I was a brakeman on the caboose. One day when our train stopped in front of your house, you girls were outside. I wanted, in the worst way, to come and talk to you but I knew I couldn't."

Not only did Mack's story truly touch our hearts, but it also confirmed two things—that the family had cared about us and that they had not lost track of us.

Later, we met Kit. She gave me a handcrafted linen chest that was created by our grandfather, Malcolm Beyer. Inside the lid, he had carved "Kathryn." Years later, I gave the chest to my sister since I was downsizing for the move from my farm home in 1986.

We also met Ray Yocum. Ray, too, was an artist and woodworker having carved a church alter as one of his accomplishments. Some of Ray's paintings were seen on Geisinger Medical Center office walls until they were replaced with more modern art. Ray, Malcolm, and Kathryn were twenty years my senior as my father, Lee, was born late in my grandparents' lives. They are now all deceased.

Finding one's long-lost relatives is like putting a puzzle together, a piece at a time. Yet a missing piece is that I never had the privilege of knowing my natural parents.

Single Again

While attending the United Church of Christ in Mausdale, I grew in my walk with the Lord. I had been asked to take a leadership role in the adult opening and hymn time. Additionally, I taught Vacation Bible School in the craft department for two weeks each June. I was also involved with the youth group at the church. One of the highlights, while attending St. John's were the "night watch" services held each New Year's Eve.

I had joined a group of other couples from the church who had also come to know Jesus as Savior. They were Harold and Jean Kapp, Paul and Helen Edmeads, Dawn and Earl Kashner, Murray and Mae Hackenburg, Marjie Chappel and myself. We began a Wednesday night Bible study in the Kapp's home. We were all growing in our walk with the Lord at about the same level of maturity. Our group became known as "the clique" which caused a stir in the church. In each his own time, we all began to attend First Baptist Church on Pine Street in Danville.

It was New Year's Day, 1978 that Lawrence, Greg, Gary, and I attended for the first time. It was a marvelous Sunday and felt like a breath of fresh air as Pastor Calvin R. Beveridge preached the gospel. I remember the pews were packed and it seemed like we'd come home. The following Sunday I attended with the boys while Lawrence hauled milk. The boys had gone to their respective Sunday school classes. I joined the New Life class taught by Jim Bowen. That morning, as I climbed the stairs to the second floor, I had flashbacks of a time when I was young. Aunt Sarah and Uncle Danny, on rare occasions, had taken my sister, cousin Conna Rose, and me to First Baptist. The children's Sunday school class, I believe taught by Essie Vincent, met in that same room. Ultimately, my sister would marry one of those fellows in that class.

There I met new friends, as did my sons in their Sunday school class. Our older son joined the youth group. His regret over leaving his buddies at St. John's United Church of Christ changed to joy as he began to experience fun times with new friends.

The congregation was in the process of building a new church in the country not far from our home on Cameltown Hill. We relocated there in February, 1979. I volunteered to help with Pioneer Girls. Barbara Wands and I led our group in Bible Exploration, working with crafts, visiting Danville State Hospital patients, and much more. I gathered up neighborhood girls to join us, including my niece, Laurie Webb. At Christmastime, we met at Barb's home. We served ice cream snowballs covered with coconut, added a candle, dimmed the lights and sang *Silent Night*. It was a most festive time and a beautiful memory.

That same summer, 1979, Lawrence and I took the boys on a trip to see the wild, wild west. Little had I known that, in a few short years, family vacations would come to an end. In the summer of 1982, we had taken a trip to Lake George, New York. Greg had completed a year at Pine Brook Junior College in

Coopersburg, Pennsylvania and was pretty much on his own. He had, however, gone with us on this drive to Lake George. On the way, we stopped in Troy, New York and enjoyed lunch at Shakey's Pizza. We had also visited an antique shop. Among the old dressers, ornate mirrors, and depression glass was a cigar store Indian. We had a wonderful time on that trip. Lawrence and I decided that it would be the perfect place to visit, perhaps year after year, when he retired. However, that fall our plans had changed.

On Wednesday, September 22 a neighbor, Spike Blue, offered my husband the sale of some of his farm acreage. Previously, Lawrence had rented the field to farm thus he was the perfect candidate to purchase the property. On Thursday we drove over to Spike Blue Hollow to walk the ground. Already warm to the idea of owning the property, we would decide within a few days.

The following morning we kept a hospital appointment that I had scheduled for Lawrence in response to a pain he'd been having on his left side. It had not bothered him through the day. But about a half hour after going to bed, he was forced to get up and sit in a chair in the living room. When he went back to bed, the pain returned.

I sat in the waiting room while he saw our physician assistant. Joanie had been a friend in our church family. After the appointment, we left the hospital wondering why he wasn't given a prescription. We had no diagnosis. However, Lawrence said they had taken blood samples. I was to assume we were to wait for a phone call. Our bookstore was open Friday nights, and I relieved my part-time employee who worked until 4 PM. The supper hour was never a busy time at the store. I used that time taking care of special orders, phone calls, and arranging merchandise on the shelves. While I was behind the counter sorting through notes, I looked up and noticed Joanie opening the door. I knew, instinctively, she had bad news. She approached, my eyes met hers, and she told me that Lawrence had leukemia. She said he was being placed under Dr. Adel Makary's care and that he would phone my husband for admittance to the hospital that same evening.

The blood count results indicated that the white cells were so high that he was susceptible to infection. The pain he'd been experiencing in his left side was explained as white blood cells clogging the spleen. I was relieved that we were assigned to Dr. Makary. He, too, was a friend from church and also taught our Sunday school class, the New Life class.

While I was grappling with the shocking news, the phone rang. It was Lawrence. While it now seems inappropriate, I looked at Joan and gestured, "Should I tell him?" Joan advised, "No!" Lawrence then proceeded to tell me he'd gotten a phone call from the hospital and was asked to be admitted. He had not been told his diagnosis at that time. Joan left the store assuring me we had her and Dr. Makary's prayers and support. I was not ready to ask any further questions.

In a blur, I closed the store and drove home. Lawrence, Gary and I left for the hospital not stopping for anything to eat. Once my husband was settled into a room, Gary and I drove for fast food and returned to the hospital. We had what we referred to as a "picnic" in the hospital room. Our wedding anniversary was just a few days away—September 30. We had already suspected that this was where we were going to spend our anniversary. And it was.

It was days until my husband allowed the diagnosis, chronic granulocytic leukemia, to sink in. "I can't understand it, I feel good," he repeated as we drove home a week later. As the news traveled among family, church friends, and bookstore customers we received many offers of prayer and support. Life wavered from good times to bad during the following weeks and months.

In September of 1983, we took Gary out of school and made another trip to Lake George. Though unmentioned, we thought it would be our last vacation. We loved the area and rented a motel with an indoor heated swimming pool. We visited interesting surrounding regions and charming shops. The heated pool was a highlight. Then came the time to head back to Pennsylvania. It had been a wonderful time; proving to be our last vacation.

Over the course of Lawrence's battle with leukemia, he had five remissions. The cancer cells had invaded his brain. Treatment added months to his life for which we were very grateful; first to the Lord but also for the medical staff at Geisinger. He had hoped his life might be extended until Gary graduated from high school, but that was not to be. After twenty months of chemotherapy treatment, even trying homeopathy and eating a more healthy diet, my husband was admitted to the hospital for the last time.

It was April 1, 1984. I spent many hours in his room helping to care for him. Night times I remained at his bedside through the wee hours of the morning. When finally he slept I was able to steal away. I remember the mostly bare parking lot, normally filled with vehicles beyond capacity. The darkness aglow only by the parking lot lights, I located my car. I may have been the only passenger in the shuttle van those early mornings when I left the hospital, and undoubtedly one of few vehicles on the road to home. I felt lonesome and exhausted.

Our kids would already be in bed; I was thankful they were old enough to be home alone. Throughout April my co-worker, Ethel Magargle, kept things going at the bookstore. I was grateful she had been trained in all areas of managing the store. I was free to care for my husband in his final days.

Palm Sunday and Easter had passed. The following Saturday

night my mother-in-law remained with me at the hospital. Finally, around 10:30 PM, Dr. Makary came to his room and suggested we go home. I had developed some coughing bug and, though I felt compelled to be by his side, I took our doctor's advice. I told my mother-in-law that I would pick up his things in the morning. She advised me to take them with me. Later, I remembered the palm branch behind a picture on his wall in that dreaded hospital room. A kindly priest had brought it into his room on Palm Sunday. It was the only thing remaining when we left my husband's bedside. Indeed, it was a reminder of our Lord's triumphant entry into Jerusalem and His victory over death on the cross. A cross that seemed so much like the one my husband now faced; triumph after suffering those long months of fighting the affliction.

My mother-in-law and I ran through the parking lot in pouring rain. Roaring thunder resounded as though Jesus Himself was shouting, "Tonight I am coming!" I struggled to recall where I had last parked. Finally, I found my car, and we were under cover from the storm and on our way home. I dropped into bed. The unrelenting cough kept me awake for a long time. I was overwhelmed with grief and concern for the boys as the hour approached.

Finally, I was awakened by the phone a few minutes before 2 AM and the beginning of daylight saving time. I flew to the kitchen to grab the phone. It was Dr. Greco. He had been with my husband in his last moments. I felt grateful. I was asked, by medical rules, if I wanted an autopsy. "No, we already know why he died." My in-laws were grateful I did not choose to go that route.

Somehow I knew I had to tell the boys. They had seen him, along with my father-in-law, earlier in the hospital. I first awakened Gary. I can't even tell you what I felt at that time. I then went into Greg's room to let him know his dad had died.

Sheer exhaustion and the persistent tickling in my throat drove me back to bed. Later, I felt guilty that I hadn't even hugged my kids on hearing the most difficult news they would ever bear. At the same time, I was comforted that I hadn't heard any sobs. I guess, by that time, the end was not so stunning and I think the boys went back to sleep.

The following morning, Sunday, I was grateful that my mother-in-law had the foresight to advise me to bring all his things home the night before. Now, I couldn't imagine going back to an empty room to gather his belongings. I envisioned the palm branch resting behind the picture on the wall. As I settled into our rocking chair I was reminded, now I am a widow. How could one so young be referred to as a widow, I thought. Little had I known that the stigma "widow" would follow me over the years and decades until an age when widowhood was more "appropriate."

More than three decades have passed. There were times, over those years, when I thought I might marry. I struggled to figure out how some single lady could simply be looking for her lost dog and, along the trail, meet Mr. Wonderful. Or, how those dreams always came true in a Hallmark movie, but for me never happened. Yet I have accepted the Lord's will for my life remembering the Apostle Paul's advice to the widow, "you will be happier if you remain single."

Gary and Conaley Visneski had shown up at our bookstore in 1983. Ethel was working that day. She phoned to let me know that she had met this nice Christian couple. They had been visiting in Danville and had planned to re-establish a funeral home in which the former director had long retired. I knew, at that moment, they would have our support. Soon they moved to Danville; then made First Baptist Church their home church.

That Sunday afternoon Gary came to make the funeral

arrangements. I decided on visitation on the evening of May 1 and the memorial service and funeral on Wednesday, May 2. It was all set. Later that afternoon a knock came to my door. It was the police. It seemed that my son had been riding his motorcycle off farm property and on the township road, which was illegal. I'm not sure how they had made the discovery, but instinctively I knew that Gary was acting out over his dad's death. I told the officer that his dad had died that morning. He sympathized and informed me that he was not going to press any charges. I was relieved.

The following day I had gone with my sons and mother-in-law to choose a casket. My husband had only two dress suits. It's a farmer thing! Since I had always planned what we would wear to church the Saturday night before, on Sunday mornings, he would ask, "Am I going as the blue boy today or the brown boy?" He looked best "as the blue boy," so I chose a blue casket and his blue boy suit.

It surprises me that I am writing about my black dress because I've always known few would ever believe it. It was sometime in the 1970s. I was downtown in Danville shopping. Passing by Cohen's clothing store a sign in the window caught my eye, "Going Out of Business." Cohen's had been a fixture on Mill Street for generations. A few years before, the owner added a new section of ladies dresses to his men's line. I backed up and went inside.

While riffling through the ladies dresses one had caught my eye. I stretched it out from its hanger, and a thought entered my mind. Somehow I knew this dress was intended for my husband's funeral. I can't explain how or why this thought came to mind. Some people refer to such instincts as premonitions. While I didn't believe in omens, I did believe in the leading of the Holy Spirit. Aside from the anomalous thought that had been planted in my mind, I loved the dress. It was extraordinary, a puckered stretch fabric, and slimming.

I knew, instinctively, I was not going to wear the dress for years. But I had taken it home and hung it in the back of my closet separate from the clothes I was presently wearing. Over the years, now and then, I came across the dress while rooting for something in the closet. Each time I was reminded, "This is for the funeral." No, I can't explain it and, even more, I did not want such a reality. Never! I can't tell why such a revealing might have entered my mind but I believe in retrospect, it was God's way of preparing me for the future.

May 1 had arrived. As I pulled the black dress from its hanger, I flashed back to a day years earlier when at Cohen's store some seed had been planted for the reason I purchased the dress. It fit perfectly. Perhaps a bit shorter than the style of the day, but that was of small significance. We had arrived only slightly late for the viewing. I glanced at the visitor book and discovered that only a few had already been there. One, as I recall, was a high school friend.

Then Gary led me to the casket. There were many floral arrangements. I looked each bouquet over but was drawn, particularly, to one spray. It was a most beautiful basket of lovely orchid gladiolas. I read the card and, to my utter amazement, it read "Hilda Weaver and boys." I couldn't believe it! The family who could least afford to send flowers had indeed sent this gorgeous masterpiece.

As I stood there in front of the casket I turned and noticed that, except for two softly cushioned chairs along the side, there were no seats for the visitors. I inquired, "Gary where are all the chairs?" Any viewing I had ever attended was set up with folding chairs. Gary simply said, "I don't think we'll need them." While I puzzled over this, people began to arrive. And then more visitors. To my surprise, the line had become so long that I suddenly understood Gary's wisdom for no chairs. Soft Christian music could be heard in the background as I stood at the foot of the casket near a small table where I had placed our wedding photo and a glass of water. A tickling cough lingered, but the Lord was giving me the strength to get through the greetings, hugs, handshakes, and words of sympathy. Among those in line were relatives from both sides of our family, our church family friends, neighbors, teachers and schoolmates of the boys. There were farmers for whom Lawrence had picked up milk and many bookstore customers. I clearly remember my neighbor, Pam, as she and her boys approached. She said, "The boys don't know what to say." They had grown up with Greg and Gary. I was touched recalling that, as a teenager, I didn't know exactly how to act or what to say at my dad's service.

In the process, I had noticed that my Uncle David had not entered the funeral home, though I had seen him outside. Later, I learned that he was not able to withstand the long wait for his turn to visit. Then one of the visitors told me that the line had gone all the way down the street, around the corner and up past the former movie theater. I was stunned!

After everyone had left, I collapsed into one of the cushioned chairs in a flood of tears. Gary gave me a report—over 400 people had paid their respects. I was awe-stricken. Later, when I visited my attorney to settle matters, he related his experience that night of the visitation: "I've lived across the street from that funeral home all my life, and I had never seen that many people line the street as I had for Larry's service." I had been additionally grateful because it was a funeral which gave Gary an opportunity to demonstrate his expertise as "the new funeral director in town." Since then his business has grown and he and Conaley have gained an immeasurable reputation.

On May 2 a memorial service was planned at First Baptist Church. My husband's casket and flower arrangements were in the foyer when we arrived at the church. Again I wore my black dress. The boys, Lawrence's parents, and my mom and step-dad sat in the front row of the church. Sharon Lineman played, "*Oh Love that Wilt not Let me Go*," on the violin, while Norm and Millie Krebs sang, "*Peace, Peace, Wonderful Peace.*" Friends, neighbors, and family members attended. After the service and our final good-byes to my husband, we proceeded to the funeral car and left for Hendrickson Methodist Church cemetery which bordered the farm. As the procession drove up Cameltown Hill, it was excruciating to realize this was the last time my husband would pass by the farmland he loved and our house. We returned to the church for a luncheon.

Words cannot express how I felt that night when I walked into our bedroom knowing I would never sleep with my husband again. I looked out the window toward the church. There was a terrible chasm between where I was now and where his body lay. I'm not sure how I got through those days, but the Lord gave me strength. If I thought all those long months of his illness and homegoing were difficult, I was ill-prepared for what lie ahead.

When my husband was going through the illness, the times he most wept were accompanied with, "I'm so afraid of what's going to happen after I'm gone." He'd repeated that scenario several times over the course of his illness. I had no idea to what he was referring. And I didn't ask. I don't know why I hadn't asked. The truth is, I knew that whatever it was I would be able to walk through it with the Lord's help.

Over the years both boys worked with their dad on the farm. When Greg was in high school he had become more independent, while Gary spent a lot of time with his dad and me. Shortly after Greg had graduated from Bloomsburg Christian School he met Penny. Penny was from Millville; they met at the Millville Carnival. It was 1982. That fall Greg left for junior college in Coopersburg while Penny attended technical school in Williamsport, Pennsylvania. At the end of Greg's first year at Pinebrook, he decided to enter the Licensed Practical Nursing School program. His classes were held in Washingtonville, a few miles from our farm. Penny completed computer training near the same time Greg graduated from practical nursing school. While Greg started work as a nurse, Penny decided on a career change. She wanted to teach.

Greg and Penny were married in a lovely wedding ceremony at our church on August 3, 1985. Later, Penny graduated from Bloomsburg University and began a career in teaching. I had been happy that she came into our lives while my husband was still living. Gary, however, had been very close to his dad. I hadn't known how he was ever going to get along without his best friend.

Two weeks after the funeral when I got home from church, my mother-in-law was in the kitchen with Gary. She said that they were going to look at a motorcycle and that, if I wanted to go along, I had to get my clothes changed right away as they were ready to leave. I struggled, unsuccessfully, with this choice as he had been saving his money for a car. But they won out; I rode along all the while knowing they would purchase the cycle. And they did. Over the years the boys had a number of motorcycles and were also experienced with snowmobiles. But I regretted the incident knowing Lawrence wanted him to have a car when he was old enough to drive.

Soon I was not able to keep Gary in school. He had attended Bloomsburg Christian School, however, he became more rebellious as time passed. Before long he no longer went with me to church. Often he went to the woods alone with his gun. I worried but kept my trust in the Lord. He'd threatened to kill himself and repeated this routine numerous times. All I could do was pray. Greg was still at home during those early days after the funeral. He was very supportive as the conflict grew increasingly intense. Every time Gary went into the woods I wept calling out, "Lord, please use just *one thing* to keep Gary from killing himself." It was a constant prayer over those grievous days as I tried to manage home and business. I was terrified. I had already lived through a suicide and, in desperation, one night I cried out to Greg, "I can't live if Gary kills himself."

The following day I was in the kitchen when Gary rushed through the back door toting his gun. He had been in the woods. "I should have done it that time. I should have done it!" I was horrified. Then he blurted, "But there was just *one thing* that kept me from it…just *one thing*!" I was astounded. The very thing I had asked God to do, He did. He used that one thing to keep my son from killing himself. I was exceedingly grateful. That day was the last time Gary had gone out to the woods with his gun.

The following days were filled with discord. While I had sent him off to school and he came home at the appropriate time, I was soon to discover he was not going to school. Then I received a phone call from his principal. Mr. Kline related that my mother-in-law had just phoned him and wanted to know what steps she should take to get Gary out of school. He told her that I was his mother and that it was up to me to make that decision. I was very grateful for Mr. Kline's support.

By now I had come to fully understand what my husband had been so worried about throughout his illness. Unknown to me, the stage was being set for conflict before my husband had even died. Until he had passed away, I'd never had so much as a disagreement with either of his parents. Ours was a family that spent Christmas and Thanksgiving together every year. To have had to face this battle which seemingly came out of nowhere had, by far, been more dreadful than the months of my husband's illness; a time when at least we had each other.

It wasn't long before Gary left home. I had been worried about him, but I felt confident he had gone to his friend's house. Then a few days later I heard his voice. I looked down the hill toward the barn and saw him with Pap. I was relieved to know he was, at least, with Lawrence's parents. But I sorrowed that he was willing to give up his home and the bedroom which had become his private fortress. Whenever I walked into his room, I regretted the way things had turned out. I longed to have him home again.

During this time Children and Youth Services somehow became involved. While I cooperated with Rob, Gary's "caseworker," I soon came to suspect that he had thought I was abusive to my son when, in reality, it was the other way around. Though Gary had never inflicted any bodily harm, he was abusive in many ways. He had punched a hole in one of the walls of our home and, on another occasion, kicked in an exterior door. By this time we had been through five different counselors. Nothing was working.

All the while I was practicing tough love. It was the recommended method for handling strong-willed children in those days, even on Christian radio. I withheld Gary's most prized possessions—his motorcycle and his Atari game—among other things. But the months of trying to find the resolution for his anger was not working. It was stealing my time, my responsibility to the bookstore, and there was the expense of counseling. I was exhausted and at a loss as to know how to handle things.

Finally one day I phoned him and asked him to meet me at Franklin's Restaurant, a place we had frequented when his dad was with us. Gary had kept his promise to meet me. He slid into the booth opposite me. After we ate, I told him that I was not making this decision because I thought his grandparents were right, but that he could come and take his motorcycle, his Atari and anything he wanted that was his. Mainly I was giving up.

Soon after, I finally allowed his grandparents the custody they wanted; giving them the right to receive the monthly checks that I had been receiving until he turned eighteen. I was holding the checks because I wanted him home. I was required to meet at my attorney's office to sign papers granting them custody of my son. I did not even read the documents. In a blur, I just signed them. Then my attorney addressed my mother-in-law, "Now you have all the joys of guardianship, but you also have all the problems."

I went to my car broken. The decision I made, after a year of grief, turned out to be the best choice. Things began to turn around. In time, I responded to my in-laws and became a part of their lives in each of their bouts with cancer. I fully understood that they had lost their only son—their only child in fact—but at the same time, I wonder how much better things might have been had they supported me instead of fighting me for my son. I also wonder how much easier it might have been for my husband during his illness had that burden not been over his head.

During that time of conflict, I made the heart-wrenching decision to sell my house. By then I had concluded that Gary would not be coming home. Two years had passed since Lawrence's death and taking care of a house became increasingly more demanding on my own. Three times over my husband's illness he had advised me to sell the house after he was gone, instructing me to move into the apartment above our store.

I was in the attic of our home the day the Challenger exploded mid-air. My mother helped by standing at the bottom of the steps as I handed her a lifetime of memories. Among them were my boys' buggy, high chair, playpen and the baby clothing I had carefully stored over the years. As I climbed the steps, then hunched over in the cramped attic, I was making a mental note. I would advise any couple, as they reach retirement, to downsize before one was forced to do it alone.

Over the time of my husband's illness, we kept a poster on our family room wall. The Scripture read, "When you go through deep waters, I will be with you. When you go through rivers of difficulty, you will not drown. When you walk through the fire of oppression, you will not be burned up; the flames will not consume you." I clung to that promise.

As a child growing up my mom was always home. I remember when she scrubbed the kitchen floor. When it was all cleaned up she'd call, "Kay, take the scrub water out." I kind of liked doing that because it always gave me a chance to "test the waters!" As I pranced through the backyard, I'd repeatedly swing the bucket up over and around my head, always fascinated that I could keep the water in the bucket. That little dance caused me to ponder God for I knew naturally that the law of gravity had something to do with Him.

My parents never took me to Sunday school or church but fortunately, growing up in a small town, I was able to walk there with my friends. We attended Sunday school, weekly youth meetings, services often, and Girl Scouts at our neighborhood church. Through all of my growing up years I had searched to know God, yet I had never heard that Jesus could live in my heart. Instinctively, I knew there had to be some way to connect. Mom always said that "If you're good, you'll go to heaven." However, I was never satisfied with that instruction. While I wasn't really bad, neither was I always good. Later I learned what God had to say about that. I continued to search for a way to bridge the chasm between myself and God.

The Bible says, "You will find me when you seek me if you look for me in earnest. " Jeremiah 29:13

As I look back over my life I can see God's hand in each crossroad I faced. He led me, step by step, until the day I arrived in Hilda's Sunday school classroom. To this day I can see her gesturing with her hand explaining that Jesus could live in one's heart. I knew at that moment that I had found the bridge that led me to Jesus. God's Word tells us "For the wages of sin is death, but the gift of God is eternal life in Christ Jesus our Lord." Romans 6:23.

God has given us a gift. He sent His Son to die on the cross for our sins, that we might spend eternity with Him in Heaven when we die. The Bible says, "Yet all who receive Him, He gave the right to become children of God." John 1:12
Jesus knocks at your heart's door waiting for you to let Him in. May today's date be the day you will open your heart and receive God's free gift of salvation.

Now, having discovered truth, I have the assurance that when I die I will go to heaven to be with my Lord and Savior, Jesus Christ. He has promised, "Then you will know the Truth and the Truth will make you free." John 8:32

Yes, there really is a Kalamazoo!

Lacking a college degree, I had a growing concern about my financial future. At age 43 I considered college, but I had been well aware that young graduates were not finding jobs nor getting hired. I didn't want to spend the little equity I had on a college degree when I felt little hope of translating that into a career. While I struggled to keep the bookstore afloat, I became increasingly concerned about how I was going to pay the bills. It was true that I did have a cosmetology license, however, starting from scratch to operate a beauty shop business seemed remote. Furthermore, beauty shops in the Danville area had by then been well established.

When the house was sold, my first aim was to pay off the $15,000 debt I owed my in-laws. It was the balance of a loan on a second mortgage. In 1975 my husband and I purchased a neighboring farmhouse on fifty acres of land. I had a personal commitment to leave this world not owing anyone a dime. To date, the Lord has enabled me to keep my commitment. I was left with a smaller amount of equity; most of which was consumed on repairs of my building at 295 Mill Street.

With the help of my church family, I moved from my home on Cameltown Hill into an apartment above my bookstore. I'll never forget the pain of leaving my beloved home on the farm. Before I left that final time, I made one more walk around my yard. I wanted to seal those memories I had enjoyed over twenty years of sunrises and sunsets. The many trees and shrubbery I had personally planted had matured into lovely shades of greens and gold. I recalled the twenty years of birthday parties, pets, and neighbor kids. I wanted to drink it all in one last time. That day was one of the hardest days of my life. Buoying me on was my husband's suggestion, three times during his illness, that I sell the house and move above our store. It was, in fact, the only thing that kept me going.

While remodeling my new home, the third-floor apartment, my contractor was removing the ancient linoleum flooring in the hallway. Underneath we discovered old Danville newspapers. I found it fascinating, having learned the approximate time when the flooring had been installed. Old newspapers, I had been told, were used as an underlayment to prevent creaking floors. It was like a trip back in time. But I was not prepared for the bold print on the front page of one newspaper. Right there in big headlines read: "Moses Stetler fires gun at wife!" I always knew my grandfather was an abusive alcoholic. Years later, when I was creating our family tree, I had read he'd spent time in the "lock up." Now dismantled, the lock up was located in the alley across from the Masonic Temple. It was an overnight "cooling off cage" for the inebriated. Mom had once told me that my grandfather had tried to kill my grandmother Bertha, but I had never dreamed I'd find the story hidden in the floor of my building on Mill Street. But there it was in black and white. I kept the newspaper for a time, but it eventually became a part of downsizing for yet another move. This time to Kalamazoo, Michigan.

In April, 1988 I concluded that I could no longer keep my bookstore going. While my husband and I had grown the business serving more than twenty-seven churches and a stable clientele, wearing all the hats became increasingly difficult. Until then, my husband in part covered the bills. Perhaps not a very professional way to run a business, but ours was just a "mom and pop" store. We counted ministry above making money. As much as I loved managing the bookstore, all avenues of trying to maintain it had been exhausted. I began to plan a going out of business sale when brothers inquired about purchasing it. Upon disclosing my records, they were satisfied and bought the business. They rented the storefront. I made certain that all my creditors were paid before the business was turned over to the new owners.

That summer I enrolled in a correspondence Christian writers course. While the training was valuable, there were some areas of writing in which I had no interest, such as playwriting and poetry. Later I enrolled in a writers conference held at Moody Bible Institute. Flying over the Chicago skyline in the sunset was a glorious sight, a treat which has remained in my memory to this day. It was a weeklong seminar. When classes ended each day, several of us women walked to a nice restaurant in the city. We had a grand time sharing each others' dreams of being published. Saturday, we went shopping in the Chicago loop.

We had made plans to attend the famed Moody Church the following morning. After we gathered in the college courtyard, we walked blocks and blocks on LaSalle Street to the church. We joked that the weather had proven Chicago's claim as the "windy city!" Finally, we reached the church and settled into a pew. We had listened to *Songs in the Night* on radio for many years and were eager to hear Dr. Irwin W. Lutzer share from

143

God's Word. The long walk back to the city was filled with chatter. We enjoyed lunch at a restaurant not far from the Bible Institute. I recall that trip as being one of the most fun times of my early widowed life. Trying my wings solo for this writers conference was a boost to my self-esteem and a springboard for putting pen to paper. My first attempts with publishers, the ones which became familiar through my bookstore, proved to be successful. I had numerous devotionals published by Warner Press, David C. Cook, Standard Publisher, and several others.

Soon after I had been widowed, I responded to a sermon my pastor had preached. He had asked those willing to commit themselves to becoming missionaries to come forward. Before my husband had passed, he had suggested I remarry after he was gone. I told him, "No, I want to be a missionary." I had been instructed that I "needed some Bible training." Thus, I enrolled in Liberty University School of Lifelong Learning. I studied Old and New Testament, having been taught by Dr. Ed Hindson and the late Dr. Ed Dobson. I earned A or B plus grades, something I had never accomplished in high school. Among other courses, I registered for a class in English literature.

While I had not become a foreign missionary, I sought other avenues for outreach. I enrolled in CLASS—Christian Leaders Authors and Speakers Seminars presented by noted author and public speaker, Florence Littauer. I had been familiar with her many books I'd sold in my bookstore.

I flew to Wichita, Kansas for the seminars. As the hotel receptionist handed me my room key, I asked, "Would you please give my room phone number to another lady who will be checking in for CLASS?" It was a Sunday, and I had time to kill. To my surprise, the phone rang in my room. A sweet lady's voice said, "Hi, I'm Nancy Dorner, and I'm here for CLASS." Nancy and I met at the hotel restaurant. She had been recovering from a broken wrist. Her son, David, joined her on the trip to assist in carrying her bags. I asked, "Where are you from Nancy?" She replied,"Kalamazoo, Michigan." "Oh really? When I was growing up, we had a Kalamazoo stove in our kitchen...." We hit it off immediately.

The first day of CLASS we had broken into groups. We were then asked to select a magazine from a table on which various publications were spread. The one I chose pictured a masked lady on the cover with the inscription: "Are you the one wearing this mask?" I had been taken aback. Of course, I was wearing a mask! Few people knew of the tragic events of my past. I had kept those memories buried deep inside. Aware that God has called us to help others when they go through similar painful events, I began to remove my mask.

In free time that week, my friendship with Nancy grew. It had been a delightful week spending time with her and David. We had gone shopping and had been especially enthralled with the San Francisco Music Box store. The following November I received a phone call from Nancy. She invited me to fly to Kalamazoo to spend a week in her home. She and her husband, Kenneth, met me at the airport. From there we attended their Sunday school class Christmas party at an elegant hotel. As we drove home that evening, even in the dark, I was falling in love with Kalamazoo.

Over the next several days we discussed our shared interest in writing. Nancy had written several manuscripts and traveled as a speaker for Christian Women's Clubs. Later, over breakfast at Rykses Restaurant, Nancy expressed her need for a traveling companion for her speaking engagements. I said, "Nancy I could be that person." She said, "Yes, you could!" It had been a wonderful week and, having agreed to partner with her in ministry, I had promised to return in January. The plan was that she would tutor me in my writing and train me to speak for

145

Christian Women's Clubs.

On January 5, 1990, having loaded my car the day before, I began the drive to Kalamazoo during a severe snow storm. I reasoned that I had the car packed and I should drive out of the storm. I soon realized it wasn't a bad decision since there was little traffic. As I entered Ohio, the storm had minimized, and I was going to make it to Kalamazoo. Finally, I passed Coldwater and continued the drive to the Angling Road Exit in Kalamazoo. Another highlight in my newly widowed life, I thought, Lawrence would be proud of the choices that moved me on in my solo walk. I settled into a guest area in the lower level of the Dorner home. I began typing Nancy's manuscripts and traveled with her on several speaking engagements. I was becoming familiar with Kalamazoo and at the same time, began to write my message for Christian Women's Clubs.

In the spring I had driven back to Pennsylvania to see my family. While I was gone Nancy recalled the music boxes we had seen at the San Francisco Music Box store. When I returned to Kalamazoo, she said, "Kay, I think you should use music to tell your story." She added, "Your life story bears painful events and should be brightened with music." I said, "Nancy that's a wonderful idea." Since I had purchased some musical figurines when I owned my bookstore, I would not have to look far for those that matched my theme. My message began with "Memories." Another prop was a replica of a Wurlitzer jukebox that lit up in bright red, yellow and blue. Battery-operated, it played mini tapes, one of which was an Elvis Presley song. It was perfect for my story which included events from my teen years. Another was a figurine of Daniel Boone. When wound, it played "Davy Crockett." "Over the Rainbow" could be heard as I related that my life began with tragic circumstances, but God was faithful. I came out into the bright sunshine with a beautiful rainbow at the end.

Gathering information, I created a message for the special feature segment of Christian Women's Clubs. Included was the history of music boxes and interesting facts about both figurine and disc style music boxes. During those wonderful days in Kalamazoo, Nancy and I traveled to such areas as Kankakee, Chicago, Crystal Lake, Joliet, and Naperville in Illinois. And in Michigan to Saint Ignace, Lansing, Livonia, Monroe and other cities and towns. Indeed my daydreams of traveling, as the colorful boxcars passed my school window in 1955, had all come true.

At the Christian Women's Clubs when Nancy was the guest speaker, I presented the music box special feature. We exchanged positions when I was the guest speaker. Later, when I had spoken at the Danville Christian Women's Club, someone came up to me afterward. She commented: "Do you see how God had planned your life from the beginning—even with a Kalamazoo stove?"

After a time in Michigan living in Dorner's guest room, I decided to look for a house. Nancy, having known the area, was very helpful with the search. We drove around checking all the areas that might be affordable. One of those drives took us to Parker Avenue. It was a charming area, tree-lined and inviting in every way. We came upon a cute little house with a "For Sale by Owner" sign in the front yard. After much thought, I phoned the owners.

In the end, I purchased the "Hansel and Gretel" house on Parker Avenue. An English cottage with a lush backyard, pine-tree-lined driveway, and English Ivy growing along a stockade fence that separated my home from the neighbors'. In time I got to know Kathy and Jerry, but who would have guessed that I would one day place their house on the market and find them a home in the country for their growing family!

147

The paperwork was finalized. I drove back to Pennsylvania to make preparations for moving into my new home. Near Halloween, I journeyed back to take up residence in my little dream house. I unloaded my car with those things I had packed and then began a walk-through. I went upstairs and peered out the window. The tall maple tree in my backyard was aglow with beautiful orange, yellow and tan foliage. At night time the street light cast a shadow on my bedroom window, the leaves dancing on the accordion paper blinds. It was awesome! I felt very blessed to be living in a storybook cottage. Lacking a bed for the night, I drove to a Sears store at a shopping center and bought a mattress. Believe it or not, I had it tied to my car roof and drove it home. Later, the box springs were delivered.

Nancy was artistic and gifted in color and design. The next day she joined me as I shopped for new furnishings. She spied a post style bed. It was perfect! I chose a dining room table with a full glass top to give the illusion of greater space. When my furniture was delivered, I sat down on one of the caned chairs at my dining room table. I was captivated by the reflection of fall leaves drifting through sliding glass doors onto the table top.

My new home featured round-top plank doors with black hammered wrought iron latches. The coat room door matched; its beauty was further enhanced with a Dutch door. In the living room was a beautiful brick working fireplace which I painted white. When furnished the house was any girl's dream home.

The time had come for me to seek employment. Little had I known then, that my ancestors were business owners and entrepreneurs. I was cut from the same cloth. It didn't take long to enroll at the Kalamazoo Board of Realtors to begin classes in the sales and listings of real estate. It had snowed the day of my real estate exam. Nancy insisted she drive me to the testing location. I never got along with math; saving all eight math questions until last. Nevertheless, I had excellent instructors and felt pretty good about how I had done. I watched the mail and, finally, recognized the envelope. I had passed!

License in hand, I had initially worked in an office in which the female employees were somewhat stuffy and mainly non-communicative. But I remembered an assistant broker at a different office who tried to recruit me. I phoned him. Larry's first words, lightheartedly, were, "See, I told you to come with us!" Thus I left the first Realtor and went with this very progressive office in which I received proper training. There were over one hundred co-workers; each one very approachable. My office mate, Joy, lived up to her name. She was indeed a delight, contrasting my experience at the former office. Joy and I had gone numerous times to Charlie's Chicken across the street for lunch. As my confidence grew so did my success. I was having the time of my life.

Meanwhile, I had joined the Kalamazoo Toastmasters Club and met many new acquaintances. Each week my speaking skills were honed, and I learned how NOT to be the "Wizard of Ahs." What I most appreciated about Toastmasters was that you were encouraged to speak about your experiences and preferences without limitations. Within weeks I had earned my first trophy. At Toastmasters I brushed elbows with a bunch of cohorts who were genuinely friendly folks. I was settling into Kalamazoo and, to this day, I can still recall the first time someone called out "Hi Kay" at Meijer's shopping center. It felt a bit exciting to know that someone recognized me in an otherwise strange location.

While my real estate career had taken off, I worked my own schedule. I continued traveling with Nancy on the speaker's circuit. That winter we had gone to Chicago for an engagement returning in a hazardous winter snow storm. I was driving. All was quiet. Below Gary, Indiana the whiteout had worsened. I feared being run onto the shoulder of the road by a semi. With flashers on, I maintained a steady, safe speed. Then it happened. Out of nowhere a car with its flashers lit appeared in front of us. To our amazement, the car had led us to the Kalamazoo Exit. I flicked my turn signal on when all at once I saw the other driver had done the same. The beacon guiding our way had led us all the way into Kalamazoo. At such a time when we felt safe, we lost sight of the other vehicle. Nancy and I were in awe at how God used that car as a light guiding us safely home.

One day, when I had gotten home from work, I picked up the mail. I was surprised to receive a package. In my kitchen, I opened the brown wrapping. There was a letter inside along with four pen and ink drawings. The letter was from a lady in Northumberland, Pennsylvania. She explained that she had known my father and had recently cleaned out her attic. After fifty years she found the drawings. One of them stood out. It was a drawing of a palm tree nestled by a lake; some rocks along the shore. I was awe-stricken because it had been an exact look-alike of drawings I had done numerous times as a young girl. I wrote a thank you letter to the lady who was thoughtful enough to send them to me. I can't recall, or if I ever heard, how she had tracked me down. I wish now I had saved the letter.

After a time living on beautiful Parker Avenue, I began to consider my grandchildren. Questions filled my mind. If I remain in Kalamazoo indefinitely, would my grandchildren ever really know their grandmother? Do I want to return home to Danville ten or more years from now sorry that I had missed all their important childhood events? Each of my two sons had their first child but there were, undoubtedly, more to come. I had deep concerns about relinquishing an opportunity to be a positive role model to them.

One day I was writing about my natural grandmother, Carrie. I recalled the day in the 1940s when Mom and Dad had taken my sister and me to visit her. We were deeply saddened to discover she no longer lived in the house where we had visited in the past. I knew I would never see her again. The memory of that day had been forever etched in my soul.

Deeply torn, I paced around the house. Already I knew I couldn't remain in Kalamazoo. A glittery career didn't seem worth sacrificing a life for which I had but one chance. As it was, I purchased story books at Meijers and tape-recorded the stories. I used a bell or whistle announcing that it was "time to turn the page." I mailed the books and tapes to little Gary. It was a thrill to send baby Charissa pretty little dresses from Meijers.

When I returned to Danville the following summer, I had already made up my mind. I was eager to let my family know my decision to return to Danville. I visited my son on the farm. As I pulled into his driveway, I spotted five-year-old Gary in the yard. Eagerly I informed him, "Gary, I'm coming back home from Michigan to live in Danville." He responded, "I'm glad, 'cause I didn't like it when you were out there." I was happy, yet saddened, as I realized how deeply he had felt about my having left town.

Until I found a suitable house, I stayed with my niece and her husband. Laurie had come to live with me after my husband had passed away and the boys had left home. She was attending Bloomsburg University; thus coming to live with me gave her the freedom to study without the distraction of her two younger brothers. We were company for each other. It wasn't long before Laurie began to go to church with me. There she met the love of her life and married Ken. Today they are the parents of a teenage daughter and four older adopted sons whom they raised attending First Baptist Church.

In December I had found the home that I felt was suitable. It was two blocks from Geisinger Medical Center which was a plus as I had planned to rent the other half of the duplex. I had wonderful neighbors. In time my son allowed me to take their dog, a Shih-Tzu named Kipper. I remained in that house for seventeen years. Regrettably, I lacked the finances to make repairs which might have included a new roof. I decided to sell the home and find affordable housing. I moved into a high rise along with my dog.

Though the supervisor had told me the building was smoke-free, I soon learned that the residents were "allowed to smoke in their rooms." Needless to say, smoke does not stay in one room. The following August, I drove to a local county fair. I ordered some French fries and a hot dog. As I looked for a seat at the tables, I noticed my cousin "Dumpy" and his wife and joined them. It was our conversation that led me to seek the purchase of a mobile home in a park.

The following day I drove to a park and learned there was only one available. The unit had everything I could want in a home. It was nestled next to a woods with a deeply embedded flowing stream. I used the equity from the sale of my home near Geisinger to purchase the trailer. It needed some cosmetics, and I completed them myself. There was only grass on the property; thus I felt lucky that I could do the landscaping. I planted a row of fifteen arborvitae evergreens between my place and the neighbor. That fall I painted the oil tank and the rear deck. The buyer of my former home on Bloom Street offered starters of the perennial flowers; which I dug and planted.

Unfortunately, Kipper was a biter. All efforts to fix him had failed. I had considered having him euthanized, but I just couldn't. Then I met a lady who thought she might be able to help. I warned her that if she came to my place, she'd be coming at her own risk. She took him for a walk. All was well until she was ready to leave. She then got down on his level and reached out her hand. He grabbed it. When she tried to free him, he bit her other hand. She did not require stitches, but it was then I made the painful decision to have him put down. Knowing I would change my mind had I delayed I took him that afternoon. Several days later I received a nice card from the lady who had been bitten expressing her sympathy.

Senior citizens can be the best pet owners because they have the time to give them. Many are widowed and enjoy the companionship. Unfortunately, most single folks are the least able to afford Vet care. While I'd love to have a small short-haired dog, I have opted out due to those potential costs.

On Christmas I drive to my son's home. Later, my family comes to my place and we have "pizza night." Santa has left gifts under my twinkling artificial Christmas tree for the great-grandchildren. We have a genuinely great time.

At times I feel the tugging at my heart for the good days at Kalamazoo. Have I ever regretted my decision to return home to Danville? If I had remained in Michigan, I would have missed taking Veggie Tale videos from the church library to my grandsons. I would have missed singing "Jesus Loves Me" to Charissa when she was a few months old. I would have missed hearing about the girls' playland they referred to as "Narnia" and playing baseball with the boys. I would have missed all the school events and going to the grandsons' roller skating parties, Charissa taking a bow at the end of the Bloomsburg Theater Ensemble's *East of the Sun and West of the Moon* and Maddie catching me on an April Fool's trick. I may not have the potentially lucrative career selling real estate in Kalamazoo, but I have something of far more value—decades of memories that are priceless.

I recall a story my friend, Nancy Dorner, shared with me one day while we were driving to Chicago. It had begun to rain. She was reminded of a picnic she had attended with her family on a dry summer day. She said, "I jumped up on the table and did a "rain dance" and, lo and behold, it began to rain!"

I'm saddened that I can no longer pick up the phone and laugh with her once again. She used to quip, "When I die and I'm in my casket, I'm going to rise up and down while David plays "When the Saints go Marchin' In" on the saxophone. Nancy went to be with the Lord this past December. When I join her, I'm pretty certain we will do a happy rain dance together.

Sometimes I think my husband would have hardly believed I even flew in a jet much less moving to another state and becoming a real estate salesperson. I am so grateful to the Lord for having led me on this journey; finally returning me to Danville and my grandchildren. To this day I am in awe when I think of how God had planned that "preview of coming attractions" in our kitchen in 1947 when I spelled out the insignia on the stove: "KA-LA-MA-ZOO!"

The Grandchildren

After returning to Danville from Kalamazoo, I was eager to get back into the swing of things living in the hometown I had always loved. Even more, it had been great to return to involvement in my church. Three more grandchildren came into my life. I was there to visit each of them in the hospital nursery on their births. My younger son now had three boys, my older son, two girls. I babysat them and never missed any of their special events over their childhood years. I also kept my commitment to be a positive role model to them and, though never perfect, I remained within the bounds of God's direction and instruction.

Sundays following the church service, I'd choose two new videos from the church library to take to the boys. Returning them, I would select two more; Veggie Tales, McGee and Me, Psalty, and more. I continued this pattern over several years. Later they joined the youth group at our church. They attended and participated in all the events including the "thirty hours fast" for the hungry. There were summer Bible camps at Harvey

Cedars Bible Camp on the New Jersey oceanfront, October hay rides, and snow camp. They attended Sunday school on a regular basis.

Though the granddaughters lived a distance away, I babysat them when my son and his wife had plans. Over their childhood years, I felt blessed to attend special events. Still in my memory box is the tea bag invitation to my granddaughter's tea party at her elementary "Grandparent's Day" celebration. Wearing her pretty red dress, Charissa sat with me for the tea. I was there when two-year-old Maddie offered, "Grammy, you can use our inhaler," when I had a cough. On another occasion, she slid down the stair steps on her behind. I should have known she'd become a gymnast! It was always a thrill to take Charissa and Maddie to McDonald's. Within walking distance from their home in Elysburg, I sat with them as they parked their shoes and played in the playroom.

One day while I was visiting the girls Maddie exclaimed, "Daddy's building me a house!" And, yes, he was. He and Penny had chosen the blueprints from a home and garden magazine. They purchased a lot in a wooded area near Pappy and Grammy Motto, the girls' great-grandparents. The excavation was soon completed and the foundation in place. In his free time, my son finished building the home. Pappy Motto, an electrician by trade, installed all the wiring including piped-in music. Watching the house come to fruition was an exciting adventure for all of us.

That year Charissa settled into a new school year. At one significant event, she wore a Navy blue dress with pink and yellow flowers for a school talent show. Maddie, a gymnast, was home cyberschooled. In her memory box are the many ribbons and trophies she won at gymnastic competitions. At times I flash back to those times on Martin Drive. I recall the day Charissa and Maddie showed me their "Narnia," an area

156

scratched out among the briars and weeds in the woods behind their new home in Slabtown. That same day we spotted a duck on the neighboring pond. The girls exclaimed, "Watch Grammy, Ducky comes when we call him!" Sure enough, to their "Here Ducky Ducky," the duck lit at their feet. I was amazed!

When they had soccer matches, I was there to watch. I never missed Maddie's local gymnastics competitions. Her best "trick" was the helicopter. She had it down to a science twirling on her hands, feet outstretched. I treasure the videos of the girls' events, including their jumps on the trampoline, and swimming in their new backyard pool. A tall walnut tree deep in the yard provided shade for birthday parties. Each celebration a new pinata was strung on a limb. Filled with goodies, whether a donkey or a unicorn, they were fat for the bursting.

In the early nineties, I had taken some beginner Internet classes at Bucknell University. I was eager to own a computer. On February 4, 2001, I went online. I had entered a world which had few, if any, boundaries. Keenly aware that I held the world in my hands, so to speak, I was eager to make new friends.

Soon I was in touch with a gentleman from Nepal. Dileep ran a Christian orphanage. He sent photos of all his children with their names. They referred to me as "Grandma." Around midnight Pennsylvania time, Dileep gathered the children. He lined them up facing his computer. Via Skype each child took turns talking with me. Some of them were very outgoing. Others were shy, covering their faces at first. One little girl said, "Grandma, it doesn't matter that I can't see because I know Jesus will take care of me."

At times Dileep was forced to move the children to new living quarters. One of those occasions was short-lived. It turned out to be infested with poisonous snakes. As a widow, I was ill-equipped to support them financially eventually losing track of them. As I look at the photos of each child, I can only hope they are doing well and living for Jesus.

Internet Dating

Sometime after my husband's death, I began to long for a husband. At age 43, I had been keenly aware that if I lived a full life, I would be alone for a very long time. I felt ready to meet some nice Christian gentleman. Now, at age 60, I still had remaining years by the Lord's will. At the same time, I was not willing to sacrifice my values nor marry someone out of God's will. I had embraced the Scripture, "Obedience is better than sacrifice."

Online Christian dating websites have proven disappointing at best. One fellow I had met was from Howell, New Jersey. He had phoned me a number of times and I thought it appropriate to, at least, agree to meet him. We planned for a Saturday. Feeling he was trustworthy, I decided to go with him to a mall. Over a slice of pizza and a drink, the ice was broken. We didn't stay there long but came back to my house. I felt safe enough knowing there was a lady within earshot living in my apartment upstairs. I could hear her going up and down the stairsteps doing her exercises as was her practice.

However, when we sat down to watch television, he soon began to fondle me. Without hesitation, I stood up and sent him straight toward the door. He squealed, "This is unheard of!" I said, "Not in my camp." I heard him grumble on the porch as I locked the door. I reported him to the dating website.

Sometime later I joined a widow's group of genuine Christians. One of the girls in the group began to talk about a guy she had started dating. I recognized him as the predator from New Jersey and immediately reported him to our group moderator. Though he had lamented, "I have never done anything inappropriate," Connie banned him from the group. I am sharing my experience as a warning.

As a member of the widow's support group, a widower named Jake began a writing relationship with me. As we got to know each other, I had hopes that I may have finally met the man of my dreams. Connie planned a Valentine get-together at her hometown in Indiana. A number of members made commitments to attend the event. Jake and I had spoken of meeting anyway; thus it appeared that this was a perfect time. We both committed to attending the event. I couldn't wait.

My clothes were packed, at least, in my mind. At times I envisioned my suitcases already in the trunk of my car. This trip was going to be the event of my life! Though he lived in the west and I lived in the east, we both had looked forward to meeting at the soon-coming group retreat. Distance in a relationship seemed not too great an obstacle for God, I reasoned.

Already I knew the rhinestone studded earrings and the jar of Night Magic perfume I received for Christmas would be perfect for the meeting in February. My excitement grew when he emailed to let me know he had purchased his flight ticket.

Finally, the days I had checked off on my calendar were drawing to a close and in six weeks we would meet.

Each time I opened the dresser drawer to add to my stash of cash for the trip I fondled the earrings and perfume. Dreaming of how wonderful it was all going to be, I thought about how he loved chocolate. Yes, the Pot of Gold chocolates I had received as a gift would be perfect. I'd take them. Chocolate brownies would be good, too, I thought. I purchased a box of milk chocolate chunk mix. I would bake them just before I left for Indiana.

Mid-January I noticed a slack in his emails. I reasoned, he's probably busy helping his son with the house he was building. Days passed. Finally, I wrote. Not wanting to be pushy, however, I said nothing about the get-together. Finally, the deadline had arrived for final commitment to the retreat. I was not prepared for his response.

Then it came. "I did meet a lovely lady the first week in January," he wrote. He would not be meeting me. I was crushed. Of course Jesus knew that I was deeply disappointed and disillusioned, and He gave me the grace to accept Jake's response. Wishing him the best, I moved on with my life. Though it had taken months for the wounds to heal, Jesus had promised that He had a better plan for my life. Obviously, Jake had canceled his commitment to the meeting, as did I. The event, after that, fell apart.

I am aware that many couples find the loves of their lives on the Internet, but I am sharing from my own experiences. After trying several different Christian websites, I became disenchanted. On reading profiles it was clear, for the most part, the subscribers' intent and values did not match mine. Much time was invested in the registration process on one popular site and, even though my age choices had been listed, the website emailed "matching" profiles of men who were very much older than me. I had been well aware that honesty can go out the window on the Internet and, perhaps, many of those on dating sites are in truth married. In fact, possibly most lacked any relationship with the Lord. I gave up Internet dating sites many years ago.

Around this time a friend introduced me to a gentleman from Allentown who embraced Christian values. He was morally upright, and I felt safe with him. My son's home was located in Coplay, a suburb of Allentown. Since the house had a mother-in-law apartment where I stayed when visiting my family, I was able to see him whenever I made the trek to Coplay.

We had dated for some time and he had given me a very beautiful gold necklace for Christmas; while I gave him an equally nice gift. At some appropriate time, I asked about our relationship. He told me that he had marriage in mind. His wife having died several years previously, he had decided to downsize his house. At times he invited me to look at houses with him. However, he had explained that his deceased wife's relatives were to be his heirs. A red flag went up. Even though the very last reason I'd marry again was money-related, I felt as though there was an "elephant in the room." If anything, I sensed money motivated him. Secretly, I found it humorous that he went out of his way to downplay his finances.

I have suspected that when my familial past had been revealed it might have been thought that I could develop mental problems, but I viewed any such notion as folly since no one knows his own future. Indeed, the enemy of our souls, Satan, loves to sow seeds of doubt and fear.

That he had been on good terms with his deceased wife's family, spending much time with them, I realized he was embracing their counsel. Soon his feet had grown cold. In retrospect, I feel

162

very blessed that I was spared someone for whom money may have always been a stumbling block.

I now live a quiet life alone, but fulfilled. I have believed that all my hopes and dreams, many having never been realized, will be captured one day when I shall forever be with the Lord. It is then we will no longer seek the pleasures of this world. Our earthly journey cannot hold a candle to that which the Lord has prepared for those who love Him.

I share this because I am keenly aware that, like me, there are many whose dreams have been dashed. We can take courage knowing that God has our best interests at heart. When we put Him first, He will honor our commitment. Far better to remain single than married to the wrong person.

While I remain sensitive to the Lord's leading, I no longer hope, nor seek, to marry again. One of the positives of singleness is the freedom to choose one's schedule without the sacrifices of companionship. I have been free to come and go as I wish and am afforded the opportunity to capitalize on my singleness.

In 2007 I met some of my Beyer cousins, the descendants of Eva Beyer Merrill and Harvey Lloyd Beyer. Among them, Harvey Lloyd Beyer III is a single man near my age. "Chic" lives in Colorado. They had visited Danville that September. I gave them a grand tour of our great-grandparents' native town. We visited all landmarks of interest including the location of the former Levi V. Beyer farm, the Odd Fellows Cemetery, the site of my former home on Snyder Lane, and the Thomas Beaver Library. When the tour had ended, Chic directed me to his car. He opened his trunk and, to my surprise, there was a large wooden toolbox. Inside were my grandfather's woodcarving tools! Each is initialed "M E Beyer." I was delighted, even humbled, to have been given this valuable family treasure.

In the fall of 2017 Chic and I met in Amityville, Pennsylvania. We visited various ancestral-related sites including St. Paul's United Church of Christ, the Old Goshenhoppen Church in Woxall, Falckner Swamp Lutheran Church, and other sites in Montgomery and Berks County where our ancestors had settled in the 1700s, having emigrated from Germany. Chic and I keep in touch exchanging letters, occasional phone calls, and greeting cards.

At the same time, I remain writing friends with a Christian gentleman from Indiana. I've never met Byron who teaches an adult Sunday school class in his church, but we have been corresponding via emails for more than a decade. We have enjoyed competitive Internet Bible quizzes and chatting on Ipad during football games. Byron is single; a Viet Nam Army veteran. He is also an Ohio State grad; me a Penn State fan. Indeed, watching Penn State play Ohio State is very exciting!

Over decades of widowhood, I have learned that journeying through the pain of aloneness is more than an endurance contest. It is a testing of one's faith. When we have passed through deep waters, God gives us strength that we may not have gained any other way. He teaches us along the journey how to help others who are going through similar suffering, loss, and pain. As a single, I am forced to make sacrifices available only to couples. Dreams of cruises, beach vacations, camping, day trips, new cars, and much more with a significant other died, in truth, when my husband died. It's easy to fall into self-pity, but I try to focus on those things that matter in the end. Someone has said, "happiness is a choice." I decided a long time ago to choose happiness—to become better—not bitter.

God's Word teaches us to say "No" to ungodliness and worldly passions, and to live self-controlled, upright and godly lives in this present age, while we wait for the blessed hope—the appearing of the glory of our great God and Savior, Jesus Christ.

Behind Shooters Bar

The house had been torn down. Perhaps it had been stigmatized and no one wanted to live there after my grandmother was gone. The time-worn barn, however, still stood on the alley behind the present Shooters Bar.

It was the 1950s. As a teenager, my friends and I walked from Riverside to Danville invariably ending up in the second ward. I recall passing by it never having mentioned to my friends that I had any connection with the barn. I had been aware, however, that I had once lived on that triangular plot on Snyder Lane. Years had passed since those days Mom and Dad had taken my sister and me to visit "the old lady in the alley," my paternal grandmother.

When I was about twelve or thirteen years old, my uncle ran Shooters Bar. However, the sign out front read—The Ellis Cafe. Aunt Mary and Uncle Howard Ellis lived in the attached apartment. One time my aunt held a birthday party for Sherry, my cousin, in a back break room of the bar. Even then it seemed a bit strange that I was close to the quaint little house where I had once lived.

I have no clear memory of having lived there, but I seem to recall a time when I was sitting in a high chair in the kitchen. I was alone. The house was eerily quiet, except for the ticking of a clock above the icebox. Sometimes I wish I could remember more about that house and more about my natural parents and grandparents. I guess I was too young. Or, perhaps, the impending traumatic event had blotted out my memory. I read somewhere that God has provided every human being a "blackout" mechanism which shields them from the memory of a tragic event. Perhaps that was my experience.

When I became a teenager, my mom would tell me in little snippets about my life before she and Dad had adopted my sister and me. "I used to take you downtown in the wagon." I always knew she was speaking about the place behind Shooters Bar. "I bought you your first pair of shoes," she explained. Mom seemed to love that she had been involved in my early life. I felt special.

"Liz always took the brunt of their treatment," she would tell me. Meaning, in part, that my mother was required to take the wagon and pick up food staples from the local charity. My grandparents were too proud to admit they were poor. Due to tuberculosis, my father was unable to work. He had been in and out of a sanatorium. He was also mentally ill and had earlier been institutionalized in the Danville State Hospital. Mom said, "Lee would walk to the state hospital for treatment, but we never knew for certain that he kept his appointments. He traipsed around the alley at night time wearing a dark trench coat. We knew he carried a gun in his pocket."

I learned much about my natural family from my mother, and there was never any reason to doubt anything she said. I've never known either her or Dad lie about anything…except maybe Santa Claus. When I was old enough, my mother told me the story that began with the family heirloom.

I was living in the house behind Shooters Bar with my natural parents, Kenneth Lee and Elizabeth Beyer, my paternal grandparents, Malcolm and Carrie, and my brother Kenny. I had been staying that night with Elizabeth's brother, Chub, my natural uncle and his wife, Grace, who were soon to become my adoptive parents. They lived on Market Street, just a few blocks from Snyder Lane. My natural mother had given birth to my sister on December 28, 1942. They had just been released from the hospital.

Grace and Chub walked to the house earlier that evening. I was along. I remember Mom saying, "Lee was fidgeting with a camera that night showing us the various parts." When it came time to leave I asked him, "Should we take Kay with us?" My father said, "Yes…before something happens to her." I think Mom had always been haunted by that statement.

Around midnight that night, in their upstairs bedroom, my mother was sitting in a chair tending the new baby. Kenny my brother, soon-to-be four years old, lay sleeping in his crib. My father retrieved a 32 caliber gun that had been hidden in a dresser drawer. He shot my mother in her left side, then fired a second time, shooting her in the left shoulder. He then turned the gun on Kenny shooting him through the chest.

As I read the newspaper account at the library on microfilm, I recall reading my grandfather's report to the police that the gun had been a family heirloom. Hearing the shots ring out, my grandparents ran upstairs to the bedroom. As my grandfather entered the room, my father shot at him but missed. Lee, my father, then turned the gun on himself; a shot fired through the shoulder. My grandmother, as the newspaper accounts revealed, slid the gun away from my father with her foot as he lay on the floor. Kenny struggled in his crib.

The bartender at what is now Shooters Bar, ran up Market Street to alert Chub and Grace. Mom said that Mr. Walker shouted, "Lee went berserk and shot Liz and the boy." Few homes had phones in those days, but somehow the family doctor had been summoned. About a half hour had passed when Kenny died in Dr. Benjamin Schneider's arms. My mother and baby sister were taken to the hospital. My sister had been spared, but was admitted "as a boarder." My mother remained, I believe in the hall, outside of the women's surgical unit. Ironically, as a teenager, I was very familiar with the women's surgery unit as that is where I worked in the kitchen after high school. I had been fully aware that those critical patients, of whom many did not survive, were kept in the hall close to the nurse's station.

My father was also admitted to Geisinger Memorial Hospital where he was placed in a room; the door armored with guards. Grace and Chub visited my mother. It was at a time when Mom was at my mother's bedside that she asked, "Grace, will you take the girls?" My mother responded, "Yes, we'll take them and you won't need to worry about them." Over the years, Mom had told me this account more than once, and I had been deeply touched by its bittersweetness. It was all so unfortunate. My mother then asked Grace, "Don't hold it against him. He didn't know what he was doing."

Two weeks had passed and my mother was showing improvement. She was expected to be released. However, she had gotten up to go to the bathroom one morning and, without warning, had suddenly passed away. It was believed she died as a result of a blood clot. Later, when I researched our family history, I discovered her death certificate. It verified Mom's account.

On the library microfilm, I learned there was a court trial. All the jurors' names were listed in *The Morning News*. The front page article also stated that they had visited the funeral home to view my mother's body. I was a bit amazed as I read the jurors' names. I knew some of them were parents or grandparents of a few high school classmates.

My father did not die. He was taken by ambulance, after the court trial, to the Farview Institution for the Criminally Insane in Wayne County, Waymart, Pennsylvania.

My mother, until that day, enjoyed needlework. When I was a pre-teen, showing interest in embroidery, my mom gave me an unfinished quilt top that my mother had been embroidering for me. I treasure the 1940s-style baby quilt top. My mother, I'm told, also enjoyed drawing. Over the years when I owned a Christian bookstore in downtown Danville, occasionally someone would come into the store who knew my mother. Most often they had gone to school with her. They would tell me about the pictures she drew. I had always longed for every bit of information I could get about my natural mother.

I, too, loved to draw. I recall that one day when I was sick with some childhood illness, I had spent part of the day drawing. Later, when I showed my pictures to Mom and Dad, they had taken note of my talent. Mom said to Dad, "You know who she gets that from, don't you?" I have never forgotten that moment, yet I had never quizzed my mother about what she had meant. Unfortunately, I had not known at the time, that my natural parents were artistically talented. I have thought that had I known I might have pursued the arts with more enthusiasm in high school.

I share all this with you, the reader, that you might have a better understanding of children who are adopted. Even though my parents were trying to protect my sister and me, I believe it is

169

always best that adopted children learn at an earlier age that they have been adopted. For one thing, it gives the child an opportunity to ask questions. Otherwise they may, as I had, live their childhood years wondering about the missing pieces.

When my sister and I had located our paternal family members I learned that Lee, my father, inherited a talent for woodworking. His father, my grandfather, had also been an artist. At one time he owned an art store on Mill Street. He also made patterns for the Danville Beaver Stove Works. Some stoves still exist and are valued as a significant part of Danville's history.

The Beyer family also operated a photography studio in downtown Danville. Family members had given me a photo of Grandmother Beyer which was taken at their studio. The mat is engraved "Beyer Studio." My father has worked with pen and ink, as well as oils. Some of his artwork, perhaps, remains in the hands of people presently unknown to me. I am, too, aware that some of his work was left at the Farview Institution when he passed away in 1964. Lee also enjoyed cartooning. I am told that, at one time, he had corresponded with Walt Disney.

Recently I was doing some Internet searches for Danville High School Class Yearbooks. There was only one. It was the year, 1935. To my amazement, I discovered that 1935 was my father's senior year at Danville High School. I learned that he had been a member of the "Hi Y Club," perhaps a take-off on the local YMCA, as it was noted as a Christian group. There was a photo of the members of the Hi Y group but, unfortunately, the names were not mentioned. I can only guess which fellow was my father, as I had been aware that he had parted his hair down the middle. There was only one fellow who wore this classy hairstyle. But most astonishing, as I viewed the pages on the Internet class yearbook, I discovered his cartoon drawings throughout the pages. It was thrilling to find his signature perfectly matching that of the artwork in my possession.

One summer day my husband and I, along with our sons, drove to Waymart hoping to meet my father. There was no guarded entrance and we pulled right up to the main entrance. My husband went inside while I waited in the car with the boys. After a short time, my husband came to the car. He informed me that my father had died in October 1964. Then he handed me a scrap of yellow lined paper on which was written— "Harvey L. Beyer." He was the gentleman who claimed my father's body and saw that it was returned to Danville for burial. As we drove away, I lamented, "For all we know, this person might live in California."

Later, on locating family members, we had the chance to meet Harvey L. Beyer, my father's uncle. He lived in Bryn Mawr, Pennsylvania and was a founder of Edgcomb, Franklin and Beyer steel company in Philadelphia. He was its treasurer until his retirement.

Uncle Harvey obviously had no knowledge there was a burial plot for my father next to my mother, Kenny, and Caroline. When we met him he told us, "I did not want Lee to be buried in some pauper's field; so I took care of his burial." My sister and I are very grateful that, in our absence, he had our father's body interred at Odd Fellow's Cemetery with his grandparents, Levi and Melissa Beyer.

It is hard to get into the minds of people who struggle with illnesses that prohibit them from ever finding financial success. My father had only one functioning lung. He tried hard to eke out a living for his growing family selling his paintings. Family members had told us that my father had been depressed over his inability to support his family. He had also been deeply affected by the loss of his childhood friend, Dick Elliot, in WWII.

Years ago I was given a letter that was written by my father's cousin. The letter is one of the most emotional and deeply saddest treasures among the memorabilia I received from family members. It's dated December 14, 1945, and reads:

I returned from overseas at the end of the war, October 1945—before I was out of uniform and while waiting for discharge orders at Indiantown Gap. I went to Waymart to see Lee. I didn't know the visiting hours or if permission would be granted – but I took a train from Harrisburg to Wilkes-Barre, a bus to Scranton, a bus to Carbondale, and a taxi to Waymart. I remember I left Harrisburg early in the morning and finally arrived at Waymart about 2:30 P. M. The hospital was like a fortress on top of a mountain – seemed remote and was. At any rate, it was not a visiting day – nor was Lee allowed a visitor except a very close relative. I asked to see the Superintendent of the place – after waiting an hour he granted me an "audience" explained that it was not a visiting day and that no exceptions could be made. I mentioned the fact that I had just returned from overseas and would be going back to Ohio to live – he noted the 9th Air Force ribbon and I did have two battle stars on it – so he relented – called a guard and gave me permission to see him for two hours. I was taken through a door which looked like a vault door at a bank – to a small room, where, after 15 minutes (I had been his first visitor in a year). He was glad to see me, that I know. He sat at the opposite side of a small table, and the orderly sat there between us. My first feeling was – that if I had to sit there for two hours trying to think of something to say that was not out of line with what one should say in a place like that, with an orderly, a silent but present partner I would end up in a cell in the same institution (there were plenty around in the violent wards of the hospital). I didn't like to mention too much of the outside world – did not know it would affect Lee. He could not tell me of what went on and how he lived there - I had a hell of a two hours – but I stuck it out – talked about the war – general things – went to the commissary and purchased him cigarettes, etc. While I was gone about ten minutes – he went back to his ward or room – brought me a small painting which was very good and which I still have. (By the way, the Superintendent had one of his paintings in his office. I recognized it at once and mentioned the fact to him) At the time I left, I made up my mind never to go back. It was the best for Lee and certainly, did me no good to see him. My visit of two hours brought back to Lee a life on the outside he was desperately trying to forget. I should not have gone, I suppose, but I was wanting to do something for him which no one could do. When it came time for me to leave – we walked together with the orderly into the corridor leading to the elevators. I turned to walk with the guard. After shaking Lee's hand, I was waiting for the guard to unlock the gate. I turned and looked back, and Lee was standing – watching me, and the tears were streaming down his face. I will never forget it – and at the time - I was certainly very – no words could describe my feelings. I went back to Carbondale – could not get a bus and had to stay in some rat trap of a hotel until the next day. I guess that when one is in such a place – a complete separation from the outside world – mental and physical is the only way out. Lee was not insane at the time I saw him. His was a wasted life.

If there is any redeeming factor in my father's final acts, written in his Old Scofield Bible are these words: "I have accepted Jesus Christ as my personal Lord and Savior." He had signed and dated it—even with the time of night. Then asked, "Have you?" I believe Jesus seals His chosen ones to salvation and that despite his sin, he was promised everlasting life. God's Word tells us: When you believed, you were marked in him with a seal, the promised Holy Spirit. Ephesians 1:13

One day I will be reunited with my natural father in heaven. As for my mother, I have no known knowledge of her relationship with Christ, but there are hints in a postcard in my possession that both my father and mother came to know the Lord.

It was in bits and pieces that I learned over a lifetime as much as I could know about my natural parents. The rest will remain a mystery. However, what had long been unknown had finally been revealed. I now know the long-held secret as to what happened that cold night on January 7, 1943…behind Shooters Bar.

Made in the USA
Middletown, DE
26 October 2020

22779736R00099